# A TASTE OF CARTHAGE

# A TASTE OF CARTHAGE

Food, Memories,
and Southern Hospitality from
AL GORE'S HOMETOWN

*Doreen Stewart and Jennie Stewart*

RUTLEDGE HILL PRESS ®
Nashville, Tennessee

A Thomas Nelson Company

Published by Rutledge Hill Press®, a Thomas Nelson Company,
P.O. Box 141000, Nashville, TN 37214. All rights reserved. Written
permission must be secured from the publisher to use or reproduce any part
of this book, except for brief quotations in critical reviews or articles.

Please see Photography Credits for a list of copyright holders.

All recipes used by permission of contributors.

Editorial development by Shady Oaks Studio, Bedford, Texas.
Articles and stories researched and written by Vicki Graham and
Lenell Portman.

Cover and text design by Harriette Bateman, Bateman Design

Library of Congress Cataloging-in-Publication Data is available.

ISBN 1–55853–829–1

*Printed in the United States of America*
1  2  3  4  5  6  7  8  RP  08  07  06  05  04  03  02  01

# CONTENTS

# DEDICATION

In loving memory of family matriarchs Lucille Stewart, Lula King, and Alene Stephens. May their legacy of good southern cooking and love of family remain with us and with generations to come.

# $\mathcal{A}$CKNOWLEDGMENTS

"For his merciful kindness is great toward us: and the truth of the LORD endureth forever. Praise ye the LORD." (Psalms 117:2, KJV)

We wish to express our sincere appreciation and gratitude to the following individuals: Pauline Gore, Mattie Payne, Inez Owens, Jerry Futrell, Liza Ashley, Thomas Stewart, Dennis and Gloria Stewart, Debra, Perry and Thomas Smith, Andrea Waggoner, Wilma Fisher, Sharon Raines, O'geal Carter, Cathy Kemp, Belinda Watts, Dolores Bowman, Beverly Gillispie and Gladys Gibbs. Your contributions are greatly appreciated. Thanks to Reverend Earl Dirkson for his spiritual support and Kevin Nichols, who came to our rescue.

Thanks also to Regina Brooks and the Carthage Chamber of Commerce, the Carthage Public Library, Carthage Radio Station Studios WVCZ FM and WRKM AM, Nashville's W.T.V.F. "Talk of the Town," Smith County Carthage High School faculty and students, news reporter for *The Carthage Courier*—Eddie West, *The Carthage Courier* and staff, and to Faith Young and Bettie Moore, who were kind enough to showcase their historical homes. And thanks to freelance reporters–writers Vicki Graham and Lenell Portman: Come visit anytime.

And last, but not least, thanks to Larry Stone, publisher of Rutledge Hill Press, and to Brian Curtis, marketing advisor of Rutledge Hill Press, for believing in our vision for this book. To the many individuals who donated recipes, "We give thanks to God always for you all, making mention of you in our prayers: remembering without ceasing your work of faith, and labour of love, and patience of hope" (1 Thessalonians 1:2–3, KJV).

# $\mathcal{I}$NTRODUCTION

The little white sign boasts, "Welcome to Carthage, TN. Home of Vice President Al Gore." A little farther along, the population sign shows 2,634. And that's how you will know that you have come to a great little town in Middle Tennessee that has a lot of pride in its history and its citizens.

It is said that getting to know Carthage is a very good way to get to know its most famous citizen, Al Gore Jr., who proudly calls Carthage home. A familiar refrain in Smith County is, "We are just what we are, no pretense." That's a good slogan for our nation's leaders, too.

Carthage is fifty miles east of Nashville in an area known as the Central Basin of Tennessee. There is a beautiful panoramic view of Carthage from the bridge that brings you into town over the powerful Cumberland River. Once in town, you will find that it is a friendly, outgoing city that tries to make visitors feel right at home.

As county seat of Smith County, Carthage is the center of the local government and business activities. It is the largest of the incorporated communities of the county. South Carthage, just on the other side of the Cumberland River, is said to have developed primarily because of the railroad. The county is comprised of varying terrain from bottom lands to hilly uplands, slopes and cliffs.

Upon entering Carthage's downtown, your first view of the stately, old Smith County Courthouse sets the tone of warmth and dignity. Whether in the beautiful ante-bellum mansions, in downtown shops and businesses, with professionals or with just plain folks, people in Carthage hope you feel cared about and important.

Throughout Carthage you will find one of the primary reasons this part of Tennessee is popular with tourists: The food! From two-handed hamburgers at the B & B Drive-In to delectable vegetables and main dishes at "the best place in town to eat"—the county jail—you'll be tempted and tantalized by some of the best cooking in the country.

*A Taste of Carthage* is a collection of recipes from the great people of Smith County, including Pauline Gore (Al Gore's mother), Miss Mattie Payne, the Gore's cook for over thirty years, and many others. This recipe book includes everything from appetizers to desserts, salads and soups to pastries, breads and breakfast to dinner on the ground. It's one of a kind . . . the kind you don't want to miss.

A visit to Carthage and its surroundings leaves a most satisfying taste—delicious and delightful! Come and see for yourself. You'll be glad you did. In the meantime, try a few of the marvelous recipes in this book for just *A Taste of Carthage.*

# $\mathcal{A}$PPETIZERS

$\mathcal{A}$ppetizers are a great way to get a taste of Carthage. A few fried sweet potatoes, some of Peggy Chapman's delicious Ham Dip, and Roberta Williams' BLT Bites will let you know you're in for a grand meal to come. Be careful not to eat too many of these, though. There are so many more wonderful courses to come!

## Crab-Bacon Rolls
*Mary Wilburn*

¼ cup tomato juice
1 egg, well beaten
1 7½-ounce can crabmeat
    flaked and cartilage removed
½ cup fine, dry bread crumbs
1 tablespoon snipped parsley
1 tablespoon lemon juice
¼ cup Worcestershire sauce
Dash of pepper
9 slices bacon, each cut in half

Preheat oven to broil. Mix tomato juice and egg. Add crabmeat, bread crumbs, parsley, lemon juice, Worcestershire sauce, and pepper; mix thoroughly. Roll into 18 fingers, about 2 inches long. Wrap each roll with ½ slice bacon; fasten with wooden picks. Broil 5 inches from heat about 10 minutes, turning often to brown evenly. Serve hot.
*Makes 18 servings.*

## Crock Pot Weenies
*Marika Pratt*

1 pound hot dogs
1 pound bacon
1 pound brown sugar

Cut each wiener into 3 pieces and wrap in half slice of bacon. Place layer of wrapped wieners in crock pot and sprinkle brown sugar on top. Continue layering until crock pot is full. Simmer on low heat for at least 3 hours.
*Makes about 2 dozen.*

## Cheese Balls
*Sadie Ross*

6 ounces chipped beef or ham, diced fine
2 8-ounce packages cream cheese
8 ounces grated Cheddar cheese
1 tablespoon Worcestershire sauce
¼ cup pickle relish
⅛ teaspoon Tabasco sauce
¼ teaspoon onion salt
Dash of pepper
1 cup finely chopped pecans
Assorted crackers

Cream all ingredients except pecans and crackers; mix well. Form into small balls and roll in pecans. Serve with crackers.
*Makes 12 to 15 servings.*

## Fried Sweet Potatoes

Sweet potatoes
Vegetable oil
Sugar

Peel potatoes; cut into strips about 1 inch thick. Place in skillet filled with oil and deep fry until slightly browned. Drain and sprinkle with white sugar. Serve hot.

*If you watch closely, you might see Al Gore Jr. taking his morning run through Carthage.*

## BLT Bites
*Roberta Williams*

16 to 20 cherry tomatoes
1 pound bacon, cooked and crumbled
½ cup mayonnaise or salad dressing
⅓ cup chopped green onion
3 tablespoons grated Parmesan cheese
2 tablespoons snipped fresh parsley

Cut a thin slice off each tomato top. Scoop out and discard pulp. Invert the tomatoes on a paper towel to drain. In a small bowl, combine all remaining ingredients. Mix well. Spoon into tomatoes. Refrigerate for several hours.
*Makes 16 to 20 servings.*

## Cheese Fries
*Courtney Blair*

1 32-ounce bag frozen French fries
1 10¾-ounce can condensed Cheddar cheese soup

Bake fries on baking sheet according to directions on bag. Push potatoes to center of baking sheet. Stir soup in can and spoon over potatoes. Bake 3 minutes longer or until soup is hot.
*Makes 6 servings.*

## Grandmother's Famous Cheese Rolls
*Leanne Hesson*

1 8-ounce package cream cheese, softened to room temperature
1 pound sharp Cheddar cheese, softened to room temperature
1 pound Velveeta cheese
½ teaspoon garlic
1 tablespoon mustard
½ teaspoon cayenne pepper
1 tablespoon horseradish

Mix cheeses until well blended. Add remaining ingredients. Mix well. Roll into 4 12-inch logs. Chill. Slice thin to serve. *Note:* This freezes well. The longer it is made before it is used, the better it is!
*Makes about 5 to 6 logs.*

## Mexican Deviled Eggs
*O'geal Carter*

8 eggs, hard-boiled
½ cup shredded Cheddar cheese
¼ cup mayonnaise
¼ cup mild salsa
2 tablespoons green onion, chopped
1 tablespoon sour cream

Halve eggs; remove yolks and set whites aside. Mash yolks and combine with remaining ingredients. Fill eggs.
*Makes 16 servings.*

## Tuna Paté

*Jason N. Spigner*

1 8-ounce package cream cheese, softened to room temperature
2 tablespoons chili sauce
2 tablespoons chopped parsley
1 teaspoon instant onion
½ teaspoon hot sauce
2 6-ounce cans tuna, drained

Blend all ingredients well. Pour into a 4-cup mold. Chill for 3 hours. Serve with crackers.
*Makes 16 to 20 servings.*

## Chicken Puffs

*Mary Wilburn*

2 tablespoons butter
¼ cup boiling water
¼ cup all-purpose flour
1 egg
¼ cup shredded process Swiss cheese
2 cups finely chopped cooked chicken
¼ cup finely chopped celery
2 tablespoons chopped pimiento
2 tablespoons dry white wine
¼ cup mayonnaise
Dash of pepper

Preheat oven to 400°. Melt butter in ¼ cup boiling water. Add flour and stir vigorously. Cook and stir until mixture forms a ball that doesn't separate. Remove from heat and cool slightly. Add egg and beat vigorously until smooth. Stir in cheese. Drop dough onto greased baking sheet, using 1 level teaspoon of dough for each puff. Bake for 20 minutes. Remove puffs; cool and split. Combine remaining ingredients. Fill each puff with 2 teaspoons filling.
*Makes 10 to 12 servings.*

## Creamy Blue Cheese Dip

½ cup blue cheese salad dressing
½ cup sour cream and dill salad dressing
2 tablespoons green onion, thinly sliced
1 teaspoon lemon juice

In small bowl, combine all ingredients. Serve with vegetables or crackers for dipping.
*Makes 1 cup.*

# Colorful Carthage

Carthage is nestled in a rural setting that shows off all four seasons in glorious profusion, and the surrounding countryside displays an amazing array of color. The country is most beautiful in springtime with the pink and white dogwood trees in full bloom. Their fragile, lacy blossoms lend a graceful air to our afternoon teas and other get-togethers.

The natural beauty of the area is highlighted with rolling hills of freshly-mowed, emerald green grass, a rainbow of gorgeous flowers and shrubs of many varieties. Visitors say they're impressed with the town's neat, manicured lawns, roadways, and even the pastures. There's no litter in sight, houses are freshly painted, and a general air of pride and caring is evident throughout Smith County.

Carthage has everything you need for a fun day of poking and peeking—curiosity shops, antique stores, and other mysterious nooks and crannies.

The Carthage Antique Mall in the downtown area has about sixty-five dealers with seventy-five thousand square feet of merchant space. And you won't be disappointed by the treasures and treats you find tucked into corners and displayed on shelves.

As everyone knows, the heart of a community is its newspaper. With only a few brief interruptions, there has been at least one newspaper operating in Smith County since its settlement, and that was said to be the *Carthage Gazette* which began publishing in 1809. Carthage was also home to Tennessee's first newspaper family: William and Elizabeth Moore.

Because it presents the local news in a responsible manner, *The Courier*, Carthage's present-day newspaper, is the best-loved information source. Its news reporter, the amiable Eddie West, is one of our most popular citizens, although he would never admit it.

*The Courier's* pages form the most comprehensive history of Smith County available. And history is still being made around here with each new issue.

And, by the way, *The Courier* also sees the important place that food plays in our hearts. There's a food column published each week.

## Layered Mexican Dip
*Martha Taylor*

1 package taco seasoning mix
1 cup mayonnaise
8 ounces sour cream
1 16-ounce can refried beans
1 cup purple onion, chopped
1 cup finely shredded cheese
1 cup tomatoes, chopped
1 2 ¼-ounce can sliced black olives

Spread refried beans in a 9x13-inch casserole dish. Mix taco mix, mayonnaise, and sour cream; spread over refried beans. Top with remaining ingredients, in order given; serve with tortilla chips.
*Makes 15 to 20 servings.*

## Ham Dip
*Peggy Chapman*

½ cup salad dressing
1 8-ounce package cream cheese, softened to room temperature
1 small onion, chopped
2 cups chopped wafer-thin ham
½ teaspoon hot sauce
2 tablespoons parsley flakes
½ teaspoon dry mustard
1 cup chopped pecans

Mix all ingredients well. Serve on crackers.
*Makes about 20 servings.*

## Fruit Dip
*Earlene Bennett*

1 7½-ounce jar marshmallow crème
8 ounces nonfat cream cheese, softened to room temperature
2 tablespoons apricot preserves

Beat the marshmallow crème, cream cheese, and apricot preserves with mixer until well blended. Chill, covered, until serving time. Serve with fresh fruit chunks.
*Makes 16 2-tablespoons-each servings.*

## Sugar-Free Fruit Dip
*Wilma Fisher*

1 8-ounce package low-fat cream cheese, softened to room temperature
1 cup plain low-fat yogurt
1 teaspoon vanilla extract
¼ teaspoon lemon extract
14 packets sugar substitute

Blend cream cheese and yogurt until smooth. Stir in remaining ingredients. Chill. Serve with fresh fruit. May color using food coloring.
*Makes 2 cups.*

*Al and Tipper Gore on the steps of the Smith County Courthouse after he announced he would run for the presidency.*

# Hot and Spicy Low-Fat Chex Mix
### *Earlene Bennett*

8 cups Chex cereal
¼ cup hot cinnamon candies
1 tablespoon margarine
½ teaspoon garlic powder
¼ teaspoon onion powder
¼ to ½ teaspoon cayenne

Preheat oven to 250°. Spray a large baking pan with butter flavor nonstick cooking spray. Toss the cereal and candy in a bowl. Melt the margarine in a saucepan. Stir in the seasonings and pour over the cereal mixture. Toss to coat. Spoon into prepared baking pan. Bake for 45 minutes, stirring occasionally.
*Makes 17 ½-cup servings.*

# Hollow or Holler?

Middle-Tennesseans have a way of knowing whether people are strangers or not. It's all in the way they say the word "hollow." We can identify a visitor right away if he says "hollow" as he asks directions to one of the many hollows around Smith County.

Of course we all know the *proper* way to say "hollow"—long on the final "o" sound—but Middle-Tennesseans say "holler," and probably nothing will ever change that.

Some folks say that the two words have different meanings and are used to differentiate between the hills and knolls of Middle Tennessee. When giving directions, they may say, "It's just down the road past the second holler."

A "holler" is where the valley between the hills goes on and on to end at the foothills, or it can continue on up the hill and then end where it's impassable. In Smith County, if it's two hills that come together at the bottom, that space is called a "holler."

There are some interesting names for our creeks and hollows: Defeated Creek, Salt Lick, Friendship Hollow, and Nixon Hollow, to name a few. If you're trying to get to one of these places, remember, if you don't want to sound like a tourist, say, "How do you get to the *holler?*"

# BEVERAGES

Southern cooks have long been famous for unique punches, iced teas and lemonades. Imagine sitting in the shade of a big tree in a cool breeze and sipping an ice-cold fruit drink or a tall glass of sweet tea. If you joined us, you might have to swat a mosquito or two, but if you do it in rhythm to the rocking chair or old porch swing, it won't break the tranquility around you.

Here are some twists on a few old favorites and some unusual dessert-type drinks from the ladies in Carthage that even the kids will love.

## Boiled Custard
*Francis Lankford*

1 gallon milk
12 eggs, beaten
4 cups sugar
4 tablespoons all-purpose flour
1 tablespoon vanilla extract

Combine milk, eggs, sugar, and flour in top of double boiler over simmering water. Heat for 3 hours or until thick. Stir in vanilla. Chill and serve.
*Makes about 1 gallon.*

## Marshmallow Crème Boiled Custard
*Myrtle Moore*

½ gallon milk
1¾ cup sugar
6 eggs
Vanilla extract to taste
10 marshmallows

Beat milk, sugar, and eggs until well mixed. Cook in top of double boiler over simmering water until very hot. Cook until custard is thickened to taste. Stir in vanilla and marshmallows until well blended.
*Makes about ½ gallon.*

## Hot Cider
*Dorothy Hitchcock*

1 cup pineapple juice
1 cup orange juice
½ gallon apple cider
Cloves (tied in cheesecloth or placed in tea ball)
2 cinnamon sticks

Combine all ingredients together in large pan. Let simmer and serve hot. Garnish with orange slices, if desired.
*Makes about 20 servings.*

## Cranberry-Apple Tea

1 cup water
3 regular size tea bags
1 32-ounce bottle cranberry juice cocktail, chilled
2 cups apple juice, chilled
1 tablespoon lemon juice
1½ tablespoons light corn syrup
1 lemon, sliced

Bring water to a boil. Remove from heat; add tea bags. Cover. Let stand 5 minutes. Remove tea bags, squeezing gently; cool tea. Mix with remaining ingredients. Serve chilled.
*Makes 8 to 10 servings.*

In the center of Carthage on a tree-filled square stands the dignified old Smith County Courthouse. This beautiful building was built in 1879 in the Second Empire architectural style. Local records show that it was planned by a committee appointed by the court and not to exceed the cost of eighteen thousand dollars. And it was to be paid off in three years!

Upon completion of the building, the committee reported that it was built with "such meticulous care that the new building will result in a stately edifice, of which, over one hundred years later, the people may be justly proud."

People in Carthage particularly like the inviting warmth of the building. After all, not every public facility has lovely drapes in all the windows. They seem to say, "Welcome to the Southern hospitality of Smith County. We are special; come in and see for yourselves."

Every political announcement from Al Gore Sr. in 1938 to Al Gore Jr. today has been made from the steps of this courthouse. In the 1970s the building underwent extensive renovation and was entered into the National Register of Historic Places in 1979. Needless to say, it is the center of attention as well as the center of town. We have fulfilled the prediction the committee made in the 1800s because we are "justly proud" of our courthouse.

## Blushing Pink Soda

2 tablespoons crushed strawberries
2 tablespoons canned crushed pineapple
2 tablespoons vanilla ice cream
¼ cup chilled strawberry soda
Vanilla ice cream
Strawberry soda

Mix first three ingredients in a tall glass. Stir in strawberry soda. Place additional spoonfuls of vanilla ice cream in glass almost to the top. Do not pack the ice cream down. Slowly pour in additional chilled strawberry soda.
*Makes 1 serving.*

## Sunny Sipper

¼ cup honey
½ cup orange juice
Juice of 1 lemon
1 6-ounce can evaporated milk
1 12-ounce can apricot nectar

Blend first 3 ingredients in medium bowl. Add evaporated milk and apricot nectar. Beat with rotary eggbeater until foamy. Chill in refrigerator. Beat again before serving.
*Makes 4 servings.*

## Double Lime Cooler

1 cup lime sherbet
1 6-ounce can frozen limeade concentrate
2 7-ounce bottles ginger ale, chilled
2 cups water

Stir sherbet in bowl to soften. Stir in limeade concentrate, ginger ale, and water. Pour into glasses.
*Makes 4 servings*

## Pineapple Shake

1 20-ounce can pineapple chunks in unsweetened juice
1 medium banana, peeled, cut into chunks
1½ cups skim milk
¼ teaspoon vanilla extract

Drain pineapple, reserving ¾ cup juice. Measure ½ cup pineapple chunks and save remainder for other use. Place all ingredients, including reserved juice, in blender and process until smooth. Pour into glasses.
*Makes 4 servings.*

## Black Cow Float

Vanilla ice cream
Root beer

Place 1 scoop vanilla ice cream in a tall glass. Fill glass with chilled root beer.
*Makes 1 serving.*

## Red Rooster

Vanilla ice cream
Cranberry juice

Place 1 scoop vanilla ice cream in a tall glass. Fill glass with chilled bottled cranberry juice.
*Makes 1 serving.*

# Holiday Punch
*Gladys W. Gibbs*

3 cups pineapple juice
3 cups cranberry juice
1½ cups water
⅓ cup firmly packed brown sugar
1½ teaspoons whole cloves
1½ cinnamon sticks
⅛ teaspoon salt

Combine juices, water, sugar, and salt in a coffeepot. Place spices in basket and perk. Serve hot.
*Makes 10 servings.*

*\* This recipe can be easily doubled or even tripled to serve larger groups.*

# Spicy Mint Tea

6 cups water
2 cinnamon sticks
4 whole cloves
4 whole allspice
2 cups fresh mint leaves
Honey, optional

Bring the water, cinnamon, cloves, and allspice to a boil. Boil for 1 minute. Stir in mint leaves. Remove from heat and steep for 5 minutes. Strain into cups. Sweeten with honey if desired.
*Makes 4 servings.*

# Tropical Ice
*Christy Kemp*

2 cups orange juice
1 16-ounce can crushed pineapple
2 tablespoons lemon juice
6 to 7 mashed bananas
1 cup sugar
10 to 12 Maraschino cherries

Combine all ingredients well. Freeze in ice cube trays. Pretty when served with your favorite punch.
*Makes 4 servings.*

# Spiced Tea Mix
*Bonnie Kemp*

2 cups Tang
½ cup instant tea with sugar and lemon
1 cup sugar
1 teaspoon cinnamon
1 teaspoon cloves
1 teaspoon ginger

Mix all ingredients well and store until needed for a quick hot drink. Use 1 heaping tablespoon to 1 cup water. Stir and serve.
Makes about 3½ cups dry mix.

# Breads & Breakfast

Walking down the streets of Carthage past the jailhouse, the City Cafe, or Miss Mattie Payne's place, you're bound to get a whiff of homemade bread baking. Can anything be more tempting than that?

Combine the smell of biscuits browning in the oven with bacon and sausage frying in a cast-iron skillet, white gravy bubbling on the back burner, pancakes on the griddle, and coffee brewing, and you've got a must-stop, gotta-have-it moment.

## Monkey Bread
*Lea Gregory*

3 large cans biscuits (10 each)
½ cup sugar and ½ teaspoon cinnamon, mixed
1 stick butter, melted

Preheat oven to 350°. Cut biscuits into quarters. Put pieces into bowl and roll each piece with sugar and cinnamon mixture. Place biscuit pieces into bundt pan and cover with melted butter and any remaining sugar. Bake for 30 minutes. Place on serving platter. Guests pull pieces apart.
*Makes about 120 bite-size servings.*

## Coconut Bread
*Devin Frost*

3 cups all-purpose flour
2 teaspoons baking powder
½ teaspoon baking soda
½ teaspoon salt
2 cups sugar
1 cup vegetable oil
4 eggs, lightly beaten
2 teaspoons coconut extract
1 cup buttermilk
1 cup shredded coconut
1 cup chopped walnuts

Preheat oven to 350°. Combine flour, baking powder, baking soda, and salt; set aside. In a large bowl, combine sugar, oil, eggs, and coconut extract. Add dry ingredients alternately with buttermilk; stir just until moistened. Fold in coconut and walnuts. Pour into 2 greased and floured loaf pans. Bake for 1 hour, or until a tester inserted in center comes out clean. Cool for about 10 minutes in pans before removing to a wire rack to cool completely.
*Makes 2 loaves.*

## Daniel's Banana Bread
*Daniel Knight*

¼ cup sugar
½ cup buttermilk
1½ sticks butter or margarine, melted
1 teaspoon vanilla extract
1 teaspoon baking soda
½ teaspoon salt
3 very ripe bananas
1 cup chopped pecans
1 cup raisins, optional

Preheat oven to 350°. Grease 2 loaf pans. In a large mixing bowl, mix sugar, buttermilk, eggs, butter, and vanilla. In a separate bowl, sift together flour, baking soda, and salt. In another bowl, mash bananas; mix in pecans and raisins.

Slowly add dry ingredients to sugar-butter mixture. Mix until moistened. Stir in banana mixture. Pour batter in greased and floured loaf pans. Bake for 45 minutes or until tester inserted in center comes out clean.
*Makes 2 loaves.*

## Banana Nut Bread
*Shirley Jackson*

¾ cup sugar
1 18 ½-ounce box yellow cake mix
2 cups mashed bananas
4 eggs
¾ cup vegetable oil
1 cup walnuts or nuts of choice

Preheat oven to 350°. Combine all ingredients with mixer. Pour batter into 2 greased and floured loaf pans. Bake for 45 to 50 minutes or until a tester inserted in center comes out clean.
*Makes 2 loaves.*

# Sugarless Banana Nut Bread
*Nelle Whitehead*

Artificial sweetener to taste
1 pound bananas (3 or 4) mashed
2 eggs, well beaten
1¾ cups cake flour
1 tablespoon baking powder
¼ teaspoon salt
½ cup chopped walnuts or pecans

Preheat oven to 350°. Sprinkle sugar substitute over bananas and stir until dissolved. Blend in eggs. Sift together flour, baking powder, and salt. Add nuts. Blend thoroughly into banana mixture, but do not overmix. Pour batter into greased and floured loaf pan. Bake for 25 minutes, then reduce heat to 300° and continue to bake until a tester inserted in center comes out clean.
*Makes 1 loaf.*

# Banana Tea Bread
*Lucy Hackett Oldham*

1 stick butter or margarine, softened to room
  temperature
1⅓ cups sugar
2 large eggs
¼ cup sour cream
2 tablespoons milk
1 teaspoon almond extract
2 cups all-purpose flour
1½ teaspoons baking powder
½ teaspoon baking soda
¼ teaspoon salt
1 cup mashed ripe bananas
1½ cups chopped pecans

Preheat oven to 350°. Cream butter and sugar in bowl until fluffy. Blend eggs, sour cream, milk, and almond extract into butter and sugar. Combine dry ingredients, and alternate with bananas to butter mixture, mixing well after each addition. Stir in pecans. Pour into greased and floured loaf pan. Bake for approximately 1 hour or until a tester inserted in center comes out clean.
*Makes 1 loaf.*

# Pumpkin Roll
*Alyne McLelland*

3 eggs
1 cup sugar
⅔ cup canned solid-pack pumpkin
¾ cup buttermilk baking mix
2 teaspoons cinnamon
1 teaspoon pumpkin pie spice
½ teaspoon nutmeg
1 cup chopped nuts
Confectioner's sugar

Preheat oven to 375°. Grease a 15x10x1-inch jellyroll pan. Line with greased wax paper. Beat eggs and sugar until fluffy. Beat in pumpkin. Stir in next 4 ingredients. Pour into pan. Spread evenly. Sprinkle on nuts. Bake for 13 to 15 minutes. Invert onto towel dusted with confectioner's sugar. Peel off wax paper. Roll up cake and towel together from short side. Place, seam side down, on wire rack. Cool completely. Unroll; spread with filling. Refrigerate until cold and slice.
*Makes ten 1-inch slices.*

### Filling
1 cup confectioner's sugar
8 ounces cream cheese, softened to room
  temperature
6 tablespoons butter
1 teaspoon vanilla extract

*Beat all ingredients until smooth.*

*Is that one of Elizabeth Wilburn's Classic Dinner Rolls that Al Gore is putting on his plate?*

# Quick Maple-Nut Bread

2 cups unsifted all-purpose flour
1½ cups unsifted whole wheat flour
2 tablespoons baking powder
1 teaspoon salt
1 teaspoon cinnamon
1 stick butter or margarine
⅔ cup maple syrup
1⅓ cups milk
2 large eggs
1 teaspoon vanilla extract
1 cup finely chopped walnuts
2 tablespoons sugar
¼ teaspoon cinnamon
3 tablespoons finely chopped walnuts

Preheat oven to 350°. Grease a 9x5x3-inch loaf pan. In a bowl, combine first 5 ingredients; stir to blend. Melt butter in a small pan. Stir in syrup and milk. Beat in eggs and vanilla. Stir into dry ingredients and stir in 1 cup nuts until just blended. Pour into prepared pan and spread evenly. Mix remaining ingredients; sprinkle on top. Bake for about 1 hour or until tester inserted in center comes out clean.
*Makes 1 loaf.*

# Black Walnut-Cranberry Bread

2¾ cups unsifted all-purpose flour
1 cup sugar
3 teaspoons baking powder
½ teaspoon baking soda
½ teaspoon salt
½ stick butter or margarine or butter flavor
  shortening
2 teaspoons grated orange rind
½ cup fresh orange juice
½ cup milk
2 large eggs
1 cup fresh cranberries
½ cup black walnut pieces

Preheat oven to 350°. Grease and flour a 9x5x3-inch loaf pan or 4 6x3x2 ½-inch pans. In a large bowl, combine flour, sugar, baking powder, baking soda, and salt. In a small saucepan, heat butter just until melted. Remove from heat. Stir in orange rind, juices, and milk. Beat in eggs. Add liquid to dry ingredients; stir just until moistened. Fold in berries and nuts. Turn into pan or pans. Bake until a tester inserted in center comes out clean, 60 to 70 minutes for large pan, 25 to 30 minutes for small pans. Cool in pan on wire rack 10 minutes. Remove pan; cool bread completely. Wrap and let bread stand overnight before slicing.
*Makes 1 large or 4 small loaves.*

## Apple-Nut Bread

½ cup pecan halves
1 large apple, peeled and cored
⅔ cup vegetable shortening
½ cup sugar
½ cup firmly packed brown sugar
2 eggs
2 cups all-purpose flour
1 teaspoon baking powder
½ teaspoon baking soda
½ teaspoon salt
¼ cup orange juice
½ cup raisins

Preheat oven to 350°. Position knife blade in food processor bowl. Add pecans; top with cover and pulse 6 times or until pecans are coarsely chopped. Remove pecans and set aside. Cut apple into 8 pieces and add to processor bowl. Pulse until coarsely chopped. Remove apple and set aside.

Combine next 4 ingredients in food processor bowl; process about 10 seconds. Add next 5 ingredients and pulse 5 or 6 times, just until dry ingredients are moistened. Add pecans, apple, and raisins; process about 10 seconds. Pour mixture into a greased and floured loaf pan. Bake for 55 to 60 minutes or until a tester inserted in center comes out clean. Let cool in pan 10 minutes.
*Makes 1 loaf.*

## Chocolate Banana Bread
*Mrs. Willie Stewart-Askew*

1 cup vegetable shortening
3 cups sugar
4 eggs
4 cups all-purpose flour
2 teaspoons baking soda
1½ teaspoons salt
1 cup buttermilk
2 cups mashed bananas (4 to 5 bananas)
2 to 3 cups semisweet chocolate chips

Preheat oven to 350°. Cream together sugar and shortening. Add eggs, 1 at a time. Beat well. Sift dry ingredients together. Mix buttermilk and bananas together. Mix shortening with banana mixture. Add dry ingredients. Add chocolate chips, mixing evenly. Pour into 3 loaf pans, greased and lined with wax paper. Bake for 1 hour.
*Makes 3 loaves.*

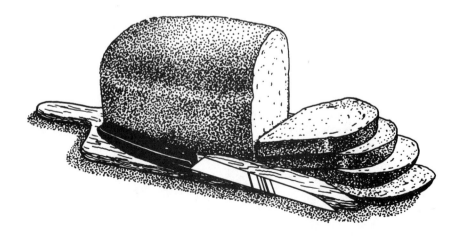

# Poppy Seed Bread
*Carol Webster*

3 cups all-purpose flour
2½ cups sugar
1½ cups milk
3 eggs
1½ cups vegetable oil
1½ tablespoons poppy seed
1½ tablespoons vanilla extract
1½ tablespoons almond extract
1½ tablespoons butter extract

Preheat oven to 350°. Combine all ingredients and mix 2 minutes with an electric mixer. Grease 2 large loaf pans. Pour batter into pans. Bake for 1 hour.

### Glaze
¾ cup sugar
¼ cup orange juice
½ teaspoon vanilla extract
½ teaspoon almond extract
½ teaspoon butter extract

Combine all ingredients; mix well. Spoon over bread as soon as it comes out of the oven.
*Makes 2 loaves.*

# Buttermilk Wheat Bread
*Nelle Whitehead*

1½ cups buttermilk
1½ tablespoons butter or margarine
2 tablespoons sugar
1 teaspoon salt
3 cups bread flour
⅓ cup whole wheat flour
1¼-ounce package active dry yeast

In bread machine, place all ingredients in order given. Select white bread setting. Bake according to bread machine directions for 1 ½ pound loaf.
*Makes 1 loaf.*

# Jiffy Corn Bake
*Nancy Hitchcock*

1 8 ½-ounce package Jiffy cornbread mix
8 ounces sour cream
2 eggs
2 sticks butter or margarine, melted
1 tablespoon sugar
1 16-ounce can whole kernel corn
1 16-ounce can cream-style corn

Preheat oven to 350°. Combine all ingredients well. Pour into greased iron skillet or heavy ovenproof pan. Bake for 30 to 40 minutes.
*Makes 6 to 8 servings.*

# Southern Cornbread

1 cup corn meal
1 cup all-purpose flour
3 teaspoons baking powder
3 tablespoons sugar
Salt to taste
2 eggs, beaten
1 to 1 ½ cups milk
Solid shortening (or bacon drippings)

Preheat oven to 350°. Combine all ingredients, except shortening, in bowl. Put enough shortening in heavy iron skillet to coat well and heat. When the skillet is hot, put cornbread mixture in skillet. Bake for 30 to 45 minutes. This makes a nice crust on the bottom of the cornbread.
*Makes 6 to 8 servings.*

# Sour Cream Cornbread
*Wilma Fisher*

1 cup self-rising corn meal
2 eggs
1 cup sour cream
½ cup vegetable oil
1 cup cream-style corn

Preheat oven to 375°. Mix all ingredients well. Pour into a greased baking pan. Bake for 30 minutes or until golden brown.
*Makes 6 to 8 servings.*

# Mexican Cornbread
*Betty Givens*

1½ cups corn meal
1 15 ½-ounce can cream-style corn
1 cup chopped onion
½ cup hot banana peppers, chopped
1 cup grated Cheddar cheese
½ cup vegetable oil
4 eggs
3 tablespoons sugar

Preheat oven to 350°. Mix all ingredients well. Pour into greased baking pan or skillet. Bake for 40 minutes. *Note:* I always double this recipe and it fills a 13x9-inch cake pan.
*Makes 6 to 8 servings.*

# Hush Puppies

1½ cups corn meal
½ cup corn
2 tablespoons all-purpose flour
½ teaspoon salt
½ teaspoon baking soda
1 egg, beaten
3 tablespoons chopped onion
1 cup buttermilk

Mix dry ingredients; add beaten egg, onion, and buttermilk. Mix well and drop by teaspoons into hot deep fat. When they float, they are done.
*Makes 20 to 25.*

*Al Gore Jr., home for a visit, serves lunch at a Carthage community event.*

## Classic Dinner Rolls
### Elizabeth Ann Wilburn

4 to 4 ½ cups all-purpose flour
¼ cup sugar
2 packages active dry or RapidRise yeast
1 ½ teaspoons salt
¾ cup warm milk (105° to 115°)
½ cup warm water (105° to 115°)
⅓ cup butter, softened to room temperature
2 eggs, at room temperature

In large bowl, combine 1 ½ cups flour, sugar, undissolved yeast, and salt. Gradually add milk, water, and butter to dry ingredients and beat 2 minutes on medium speed of electric mixer, scraping bowl occasionally. Add 1 egg and ½ cup flour. Beat 2 minutes high speed, scraping bowl occasionally. With a spoon, stir in enough additional flour to make a soft dough. Grease top; cover tightly and refrigerate for 2 to 24 hours.

Punch dough down; turn out onto lightly floured surface. Shape into wreaths for Christmas dinner as follows: Roll ropes to 16-inch lengths. Fold each rope in half and twist 7 to 8 times. Form into rings and pinch ends to seal. Place rolls about 2 inches apart on greased baking sheets. Cover and let rise in warm, draft-free place until doubled in size (20 to 40 minutes). Preheat oven to 375°. Bake for 15 to 20 minutes, until golden brown.
*Makes 2 to 3 dozen.*

# Where Everybody Knows Your Name

Al Gore Sr. didn't hesitate to tell his friends that his favorite food in the whole world was fried chicken, and the best place to get it was the City Cafe. Rosie Cannon, owner of the City Cafe for five years during the Gore Sr. era, recalls Senator Gore "eating all the time at the City Cafe and always having the chicken."

When Mrs. Gore Sr. was hospitalized at the Smith County Hospital on her birthday, Rosie fried a chicken and took it to her in her room. "Al Jr. never forgets my name either," Rosie says, "but I know it's really the fried chicken he's remembering." Rosie has been in the restaurant business all her life, but she recently sold the City Cafe to Loretta Overstreet, who is carrying on the tradition of a buffet of mouth-watering Middle-Tennessee favorites.

At lunch time the City Cafe is as busy as a beehive. The array of Formica tables and a wall lined with booths are all filled with hungry people. On the right is the day's spread: succulent fried chicken, boiled cabbage, fried okra, yeast rolls, gravy, and, of course, "beans and taters" (Loretta's favorite). Another showcase reveals a variety of tempting homemade cream and fruit pies.

How does someone decide which foods to choose? Loretta's solution is simple: Each person chooses several vegetables and salads and shares them with lunch mates. That way for $2.75 you can have as many entrees, vegetables and desserts as you want.

"Split it up, that's the key," says Loretta. Lunch customers busily engage in talking and sampling one another's foods just like family.

If you sit at the City Cafe long enough, you'll see almost everybody in town. Breaking news is told at the cafe before it hits the streets. Big political announcements, like Al Gore Sr.'s bid for the U.S. Senate and Al Gore Jr.'s try for the presidency in 1988, were whispered across tables at the City Cafe long before the news became public.

In many ways, the City Cafe is the Carthage version of *Cheers!*—"where everybody knows your name." It's a homey, welcoming place.

# Quick-and-Easy Yeast Rolls

1 package active dry yeast
¾ cup warm water
2 tablespoons sugar
2 tablespoons vegetable oil
1 egg
2½ to 2¾ cups self-rising flour, divided
Soft butter or margarine

Dissolve yeast in water in a 2½-quart bowl. Add sugar, oil, and egg. Stir to dissolve sugar. Stir in 1 cup flour until smooth. Place in warm place and let rise (about 15 minutes). Stir down the batter and add remaining 1½ cups flour. Stir until mixed and turn onto floured board and knead 3 minutes. (If sticky add ¼ cup flour.) Shape quickly into rolls; place in greased pan and brush top with butter. Put in warm place and let rise for 25 minutes. Preheat oven to 425°, bake for 12 to 15 minutes, or until light brown. Brush tops with soft butter.
*Makes 10 to 12 rolls.*

# Corn Fritters

1 cup all-purpose flour
2 eggs
½ cup milk
1 teaspoon vegetable oil
1 16-ounce can kernel corn

Preheat oil in deep fryer to 375°. Mix all ingredients well. Spoon batter into the hot oil and fry; when brown and crisp on one side, turn over. When fritters are done, remove from oil and drain on paper towel. Serve hot with syrup and butter.
*Makes 4 to 6 servings.*

# Breakfast Muffins
*Susie George*

1 egg
½ cup sugar
¼ cup vegetable oil
¼ cup milk
1 teaspoon vanilla extract
1 cup self-rising flour

Preheat oven to 325°. In large mixing bowl, beat egg and sugar until fluffy. Add oil, milk, and vanilla extract. Stir in flour. Spoon into muffin cups and bake for 15 to 20 minutes or until lightly browned. *Note:* For a variety, add ½ cup chocolate chips or your choice of fruit such as bananas or cooked peaches, or apples with cinnamon.
*Makes 6 to 8 muffins.*

# Southern Pecan Biscuits

¾ cup cold, mashed, cooked sweet potatoes
1 stick butter or margarine, melted and cooled
2 tablespoons light brown sugar
½ cup milk
2 cups unsifted self-rising all-purpose flour
½ cup chopped pecans

Preheat oven to 400°. Combine sweet potatoes, butter, and brown sugar. Stir in milk until smooth. Add flour and stir until moistened. Add pecans to dough.

Turn dough out onto lightly floured surface; knead a few times. Roll dough to ½-inch thickness. Cut with floured, 2-inch biscuit cutter. Bake on lightly greased baking sheet for 15 to 18 minutes.
*Makes about 1½ dozen biscuits.*

# Cheddar Corn Meal Muffins

1½ cups unsifted all-purpose flour
½ cup yellow corn meal
1 tablespoon baking powder
½ teaspoon salt
Pinch of cayenne pepper
1 large egg
1 cup milk
½ stick butter or margarine, melted
1¼ cups coarsely grated sharp Cheddar
   cheese

Preheat oven to 425°. Grease 12 muffin cups.

In a bowl, blend flour, corn meal, baking powder, salt, and cayenne. Beat egg with milk and butter and add to dry ingredients. Stir until thoroughly moistened.

Stir in 1 cup of cheese and spoon batter into muffin cups. Sprinkle about 1 teaspoon of the remaining cheese over each muffin and bake for 15 to 20 minutes. Serve hot with butter or freeze and reheat before serving.
*Makes 12 regular size muffins.*

# Buttermilk Corn Meal Muffins

1½ cups yellow or white corn meal
½ cup unsifted all-purpose flour
1 tablespoon sugar, optional
4 teaspoons baking powder
½ teaspoon salt
½ stick butter or margarine
¾ cup buttermilk
2 large eggs

Preheat oven to 425°. Grease 12 muffin cups.

Combine dry ingredients and stir to blend. Melt butter. Remove from heat; stir in buttermilk and eggs. Stir butter mixture into dry ingredients and blend until well moistened. Spoon into muffin cups and bake until lightly browned, 15 to 20 minutes. Let stand 5 minutes before removing muffins from tin.
*Makes 12 regular size muffins.*

# Rich Lemon Muffins

2 cups unsifted all-purpose flour
½ cup plus 2 tablespoons sugar
1 tablespoon baking powder
1 teaspoon salt
1 stick butter or margarine
½ cup fresh lemon juice
2 large eggs
2 tablespoons finely grated lemon rind

Preheat oven to 400°. Grease 12 muffin cups.

Combine flour, ½ cup sugar, baking powder, and salt; blend well. Melt butter. Remove from heat and stir in lemon juice, eggs, and lemon rind. Stir egg mixture into dry ingredients and blend until well moistened.

Spoon into muffin cups; sprinkle top of batter with remaining 2 tablespoons of sugar. Bake until lightly browned, 15 to 20 minutes.
*Makes 12 regular size muffins.*

Many older homes in and around Smith County are being restored, such as this lovely home in Gordonsville.

# Cinnamon Rolls
*Lisa Kemp Harville*

3 tablespoons butter
¼ cup pancake syrup
¼ cup firmly packed brown sugar
¼ cup chopped pecans
¼ teaspoon cinnamon
1 large can biscuits (10)

Preheat oven to 400°. Melt butter in baking pan in the oven. Remove from oven and stir in next 5 ingredients. Place biscuits on top. Bake for 15 minutes or until browned. Let stand 5 minutes. Invert onto serving tray and enjoy.
*Makes 10 servings.*

# Chili-Corn Fritters

1 cup all-purpose flour
2 teaspoons baking powder
½ teaspoon salt
¼ teaspoon pepper
1 tablespoon vegetable shortening, melted
3 eggs, beaten
½ cup milk
1 teaspoon sugar
1 4-ounce can chopped green chilies
2 cups cooked corn, drained
Bottled taco sauce

Preheat oil in deep fryer to 375°. In medium bowl, combine flour, baking powder, salt, and pepper. Stir in shortening, eggs, milk, sugar, green chilies, and corn. Beat well. Drop by cupfuls into hot fat and fry until browned. Drain on paper towels. Serve with taco sauce.
*Note:* Make sure fat is at 375° each time before dropping batter.
*Makes 6 to 8 servings.*

# Debra Smith's Blackberry Pancakes

1 egg
2 cups milk
1½ cups self-rising flour
¼ cup vegetable oil
Blackberry syrup
Whipped Cream

Beat egg in large bowl. Add milk and gradually stir in flour. Add oil and gently stir until well blended. Let stand about 5 minutes.

Spoon the batter onto a greased, pre-heated griddle. Cook for about 2 minutes, flip, and cook for about 1 minute on the other side. Serve hot with blackberry syrup and whipped cream.
*Makes about 12 4-inch pancakes.*

**Blackberry Syrup**

2 cups fresh blackberries
1 cup water
2 cups sugar
⅓ cup cornstarch
Water

In large saucepan, combine first three ingredients. Bring to a boil, and cook about ten minutes. Dissolve cornstarch in a small amount of cold water. Pour into syrup mixture. Reduce heat and simmer, stirring until well blended, about 2 minutes.

*Note:* If blackberries are not in season, substitute heated blackberry jam.
*Makes about 2 cups.*

# Saving History and Making History

The person who can describe current events of Carthage and the historical path that got us here the best is Jerry Futrell. This knowledgeable and friendly town leader has his finger on the pulse of the town.

Futrell served Carthage as its pharmacist for thirty-seven years. And now for nine years, he has served as Smith County Memorial Hospital's administrator. Why does he love Smith County so much? He says it's the uniqueness of the town and its wonderful people.

"There's a quality of people here in whom the old Southern charm really shows," he says. "This quality is difficult to duplicate. We have the old ways of hospitality, but we're also modern."

Jerry's current concern as a civic leader is in retaining the personality of Carthage, despite the influx of journalists and tourists seeking information on our most famous citizen. Jerry was one of Al Gore Sr.'s closest friends for most of a lifetime, and he remains a confidante and friend of Mrs. Gore, Al Jr., and the family.

"This is an opportunity for our community to shine," Futrell says regarding the 2000 presidential campaign. "We are totally committed to 'Little Al' (as he's known here). It's kind of like a ham-and-eggs breakfast," Jerry says. "The chicken can be just an occasional contributor, but the hog has to be totally committed."

Jerry was vice mayor of Carthage for several years. He laughs at his only tribute from our town. "Most leaders get a street named after them. This town's so old, there's no streets left to name. So the City Council named an *alley* after me!" Sure enough, Futrell Alley runs north and south just a half-block off Courthouse Square—and that's appropriate since he's credited by many with saving the old courthouse several years ago when there was a movement afoot to tear it down.

"Saving history and making history," says Jerry, "is something we need to constantly keep in mind here in Carthage, because changing times are upon us. We always want to be just what we are and not put on a different face just because reporters have come to town. I think every visitor here will be received as graciously as we've always treated our visitors."

# Mrs. Pauline Gore's Biscuits
*Pauline Gore*

> Al was an enthusiastic high school football player, being captain of his team in his senior year. For breakfast before playing a game, he wanted steak, biscuits, and white gravy.

⅓ cup solid shortening
2 cups self-rising flour
1 tablespoon baking powder
¾ cup buttermilk

Preheat oven to 450°. Mix shortening, flour, and baking powder together. Make a well in the center and pour in buttermilk. Stir just until dough forms a ball. On a lightly floured surface, knead dough gently; pat or roll out to a ½-inch thickness. Cut with 2½-inch cutter. Bake for 10 to 12 minutes or until golden.
*Makes 10 biscuits.*

# Mama's Biscuits

2 cups self-rising flour, divided
⅓ cup vegetable shortening
¾ cup milk

Preheat oven to 425°. Place 1¾ cups flour into medium bowl. Cut shortening into flour by using side of tablespoon. Pour in milk and blend well with spoon. Dust wooden board with remaining ¼ cup flour. Place dough on board and knead only enough to be sure ingredients are well combined. (It's best to handle dough as little as possible.) Roll out dough about ⅜-inch thick on floured dough board (or used wax paper or pastry cloth). With a 2-inch biscuit cutter or juice glass, cut out biscuits. Put on lightly greased cookie sheet. Bake 12 to 14 minutes or until golden brown.
*Makes about 12 biscuits.*

# Down-Home Cheese Biscuits

2 cups all-purpose flour
4 teaspoons baking powder
1 to 1½ cups finely grated Cheddar cheese, divided
¼ cup vegetable shortening
¼ cup butter or margarine
⅔ cup milk

Preheat oven to 425°. In a large bowl, mix together flour, baking powder, and ½ cup cheese. Add shortening and butter; cut into flour mixture with two knives or pastry blender until mixture resembles coarse meal. Make a well in center, pour in milk and stir with a fork just until dough forms a ball. On a lightly floured board, knead dough lightly, about 15 times, until it is smooth. Roll out dough to ½-inch thickness. Cut with a 2-inch cookie cutter or glass. Place on greased cookie sheet and bake for about 10 minutes. Remove from oven. Sprinkle tops of biscuits generously with grated cheese. Return to oven and continue baking until cheese is completely melted, about 3 minutes. Serve warm.
*Makes about 12 biscuits.*

# Funnel Cakes

2 cups milk
2 eggs
½ teaspoon baking powder
Pinch of salt
Enough flour to make a thin batter
   (about 2½ cups)
Honey
Confectioner's sugar

Beat the eggs well. Add milk. Sift salt and baking powder into a little flour. Add to the egg-milk mixture. Continue adding flour until you have a thin batter. Have hot fat ½ to 1 inch deep in pan. Put batter into funnel and then into hot fat, beginning in the center of the pan and turning the stream around in a gradually increasing circle being careful not to overlap batter. Fry to a golden brown and serve with honey or sprinkle with confectioner's sugar.
*Makes 6 to 12 cakes, depending on size.*

# Early-to-Rise Egg Sausage Casserole
*Deanna Shoulders*

8 slices bread, cubed and trimmed
2 cups grated cheese
2 pounds pork sausage, browned and drained
4 to 6 eggs, beaten
2½ cups milk
¾ teaspoon dry mustard
1 10½-ounce can cream of mushroom soup
½ cup milk

Place bread cubes in a greased 9x13-inch pan. Sprinkle with cheese; top with browned sausage. Blend eggs, milk, and mustard; pour over browned sausage. Refrigerate several hours or overnight. When ready to serve, preheat oven to 300°. Blend soup and milk; pour over casserole. Bake for 1½ hours.
*Makes 4 to 6 servings.*

# Champs Sausage Without Guilt
*Cynthia Woodmore*

1 egg white, slightly beaten
⅓ cup onion, finely chopped
¼ cup finely snipped, dried apples *or*
½ cup finely chopped fresh Red Delicious
   apples
¼ cup seasoned bread crumbs
2 tablespoons snipped fresh parsley
½ teaspoon sea salt
½ teaspoon sage
¼ teaspoon nutmeg
¼ teaspoon black pepper
⅛ teaspoon cayenne pepper
½ pound lean ground turkey breast

In a medium bowl, combine the egg white, onion, apples, bread crumbs, parsley, sea salt, sage, nutmeg, black pepper, and cayenne pepper. Add the ground turkey and mix well.

Shape the mixture into 8 or 9 2-inch patties. Preheat grilling machine and place patties on the grill 2 at a time. Cook for 15 minutes or until meat is no longer pink and the juices run clear.
*Makes 8 to 9 patties.*

# Scrambled Eggs

3 tablespoons margarine
9 eggs
1 cup milk, cream or water
¾ teaspoon salt
⅛ teaspoon pepper

Melt the margarine in a skillet; lower the heat. Beat the eggs until the yolks and whites are mixed. Then add the milk, salt and pepper, and stir well. Pour eggs into the skillet; cook until creamy in consistency, constantly stirring and scraping from the bottom and sides of the skillet. Serve with or without toast.

**Variations**:

*Scrambled Eggs and Bacon*: Cook 6 bacon slices until crisp. Dice and add to the eggs.

*Scrambled Eggs with Cheese*: Add ½ cup grated cheese and 1 tablespoon minced parsley to egg mixture just before cooking.

*Scrambled Eggs and Ham*: Add ½ to 1 cup minced ham or other cooked meat to the eggs just before cooking.

*Scrambled Eggs with Onions and Tomatoes*: Follow recipe for Scrambled Eggs, cooking 1 small onion, minced, and 3 medium tomatoes, diced, in the margarine until quite tender. Add remaining ingredients and cook until done. *Makes 6 servings.*

# Jalapeño Squares
*Crelious Sadler*

10 Jalapeño peppers, seeded and chopped
10 eggs, beaten
1½ cups grated Cheddar cheese

Preheat oven to 325°. Arrange jalapeño peppers on a greased 9x13-inch pan. Pour eggs over top. Sprinkle with cheese. Bake for 20 minutes. Cool and cut into squares. *Makes 10 servings.*

# SOUPS, STEWS AND GUMBOS

Soup's on! Who hasn't called out those familiar words? The wonderful soups, stews and gumbos from Carthage will have you ladling up soup as your entire meal. Soup crosses all ages and cultures. Is there anyone who can't sit down to a bowl of thick, steaming vegetable soup? Southern soups, in particular, are so hearty and fresh that with a big bowl of it, a slab of cornbread and a glass of iced tea the person eating is happy and satisfied.

If you drop by Carthage in time for the Smith County Fall Heritage Festival, you just might get a chance to taste Dennis Stewart's Steak Soup or Peggy Chapman's Potato and Onion Soup.

# Smith County Fall Heritage Festival

On the first Saturday in October the event of the season begins in Carthage. It's the Smith County Fall Heritage Festival held on the downtown square. Surrounded by beautiful fall colors, everybody brings their aluminum lawn chairs and lines up to watch and listen to the good old mountain music. There's something for everyone at the Festival—horse-drawn buggy rides, pony rides, antique cars and tractors, music—lots of music!—antiques, handmade crafts and, of course, food! All kinds of food, from barbecue ribs and potato salad to crunchy fried chicken and buttery corn-on-the-cob. Gnaw on a turkey leg as you stroll along among the vendors. Or sit in the shade and crunch a giant Sno-Biz Shave Ice. All in all, the Fall Festival takes us back to our roots and remembrances—a time to celebrate where we came from and where we're headed.

## Loaded Potato Soup
*Connie Massey*

4 potatoes
6 tablespoons margarine
¼ cup onion, chopped
2 tablespoons all-purpose flour
2 cups milk
2 cups chicken broth
¼ cup carrots, grated
¼ cup celery, chopped
1 teaspoon salt
1 teaspoon pepper
½ to 1 cup Velveeta cheese
2 to 3 tablespoons bacon bits

Peel and cube potatoes. Boil until tender. Drain and set aside. In separate saucepan, melt margarine. Cook onion in margarine until clear. Add flour and stir well. Add milk, chicken broth, carrots, celery, salt, and pepper. Simmer until mixture thickens, stirring frequently. Add cheese and stir until melted. Add cooked potatoes and bacon bits. Let set on low heat for 5 to 10 minutes.
*Makes 4 servings.*

## Potato and Onion Soup
*Peggy Chapman*

4 medium potatoes
3 medium onions, thinly sliced
8 cups water
1 tablespoon salt
3 tablespoons butter
2 sprigs fresh parsley, chopped

Place potatoes, onions, water, and salt in a large saucepan. Bring to a boil and then simmer for 45 minutes, partially covered. The vegetables should be tender by the end of that time. Mash the vegetables while in the soup. Just prior to serving, add the butter and stir until it is completely melted. Sprinkle chopped parsley over the top and serve.
*Makes 4 servings.*

## Cucumber Potato Soup

4 medium potatoes, peeled and diced
1 teaspoon salt
2 cups water
1 medium cucumber, peeled, seeded, and diced
¼ teaspoon white pepper
1 cup heavy cream or milk
½ cup milk
1 green onion, sliced
1 teaspoon dried dill weed *or*
1 tablespoon chopped fresh dill
Salt and pepper to taste

In a large saucepan, cook potatoes in salted water until very soft. Place sieve over a large bowl. Pour potatoes and liquid into sieve and force potatoes through. Return to saucepan. Stir in cucumber, pepper, cream, milk, and onion. Simmer gently for about 5 minutes or until cucumber is tender. Add dill, salt, and pepper. Serve hot or cold.
*Makes 4 servings.*

# Onion Soup
### *Kathy Brooks*

4 pounds onions, sliced
1 stick butter
1 tablespoon all-purpose flour
1 tablespoon paprika
3 envelopes Lipton onion soup mix
Salt and pepper to taste
French bread
Mozzarella cheese

Sauté onions in large soup pot in butter 20 minutes. Add flour and paprika. While onions simmer, in second pot, prepare soup mix according to package. Add to first pot and simmer for 2 hours. Add salt and pepper to taste. Refrigerate overnight or freeze.

*To serve:* Heat soup; fill bowls. Top with French bread and mozzarella cheese. Place under broiler and brown until bubbly. Enjoy!
*Makes 6 to 8 servings.*

# Steak Soup
### *Dennis Stewart*

1½ pounds steak, cubed
4 tablespoons butter
1 16-ounce can tomatoes, diced
3 tablespoons beef base
1 teaspoon salt
1 teaspoon pepper
1 10-ounce package frozen mixed vegetables
1 cup celery, chopped
1 cup onion, chopped
1 cup carrots, chopped
1 stick soft margarine
1½ tablespoons all-purpose flour
2 cups water
1 10-ounce package frozen mixed vegetables

Brown steak in 4 tablespoons butter. Add 6 cups water, tomatoes, beef base, salt, and pepper. Bring to a boil, cover, and reduce heat. Simmer for 30 minutes. Add mixed vegetables, celery, onion, and carrots. Continue to simmer, covered, for 30 minutes. Melt 1 stick margarine and stir in flour. Gradually blend in 2 cups water. Add to meat and vegetables; mix well; cook, and stir until mixture is thick and bubbly.
*Makes 8 to 10 servings.*

# Brunswick Stew
*Debra Smith*

1 5-pound stewing chicken, cut up
6 cups water
2 bay leaves
2 teaspoons salt
½ teaspoon pepper
4 slices bacon, cut into ½-inch pieces
2 medium onions, sliced and separated into rings
2 medium potatoes, peeled and cubed
1 16-ounce can whole tomatoes (undrained), cut up
1 8-ounce can whole kernel golden corn, drained
1 cup frozen lima beans
1 tablespoon Worcestershire sauce
1 20-ounce can pork and beans in tomato sauce
2 tablespoons chopped fresh parsley, optional

In a 6-quart Dutch oven, combine chicken, water, bay leaves, salt, and pepper. Over high heat, heat to boiling. Reduce heat to low; simmer, covered for 2½ hours or until tender. Strain broth; skim fat. Reserve 4 cups broth (add water to equal 4 cups). Discard bay leaves. When cool, remove chicken from bones; cut up chicken.

In same Dutch oven, cook bacon until crisp. Drain on paper towels and set aside. Spoon off all but 2 tablespoons drippings. Add onions; cook until tender, stirring often. Stir in potatoes, tomatoes, corn, lima beans, Worcestershire sauce, reserved broth, and chicken. Heat to boiling. Reduce heat; simmer, uncovered, for 30 minutes. Stir in pork and beans. Simmer, uncovered, 30 minutes longer. Stir in bacon. Add parsley, if desired.
*Makes 12 servings.*

# Crab-Shrimp Gumbo
*Wandelyn Dominkic*

6 cups chicken broth
3 cups canned or fresh tomatoes
2 tablespoons parsley, chopped
1 cup celery, sliced
4 tablespoons margarine
1 cup sweet green pepper, chopped
1 hot pepper
3 large onions, chopped
2 cloves garlic, finely chopped
1 10-ounce package frozen okra or
1 pound fresh okra, cut into ¾-inch lengths
1 pound shrimp, cleaned and cut in halves
1 10-ounce package frozen Alaskan crab
8 drops of Tabasco sauce

Pour broth into 5-quart Dutch oven. Add tomatoes, parsley, and celery. Heat margarine in skillet; add peppers, onion, garlic, and okra. Cover and cook, without stirring, until onion is soft but not browned. Add mixture to broth. Add all other ingredients, except seafood and Tabasco. Heat to boiling; lower heat and simmer, covered, 2 to 2½ hours.

Stir in seafood and Tabasco and cook an additional 15 minutes. May be served over hot rice.
*Makes 10 to 12 servings.*

# Classic Car Show

Turquoise-and-white '57 Chevy with whitewall tires

Pink-and-white Thunderbird convertible

When was the last time you sat in a turquoise-and-white '57 Chevy? Or looked under the hood of a pink-and-white Thunderbird convertible? Or took a ride in a Model T Ford? Well, you can do all these things and lots more at the annual Classic Car Show each June. Run your hands over the vinyl seats, tune in the A.M. radio, or check out the fuzzy dice hanging from the rearview mirrors.

Scores of classic beauties and their owners are just waiting for the lookers and longers so they can talk about their treasured antiques. It's fun to reminisce about the days of glass packs, white-walled tires, and non-computerized engines that could be fixed or fancied-up by self-taught, shade-tree mechanics.

Car buffs can also check out the Defeated Creek Auto Jam held on Sundays in May near the Defeated Creek Marina. Cars, trucks, lawn mowers, go carts and food in a fleamarket-type atmosphere lure shoppers to plunk down their money for treats and treasures.

Those who love smaller motors haven't been left out of the annual events either. Power Equipment Day is held every May in Ivy-Agee Park. This all-day event features crafts, music, food, mower and equipment displays . . . and lawn mower races!

## Spicy Seafood Gumbo
*Glenda Gibbs*

**Roux**
2 cups peanut oil
2 ½ cups all-purpose flour

If you have never made a roux, heat oil on low heat, add flour. Cook until a dark brown. Cook on low heat for about 45 minutes to 1 hour. Stir so it does not burn.

**Gumbo**
1 large onion, diced
1 medium green pepper, diced
1 cup diced celery
3 tablespoons garlic, crushed
2 cups sliced okra, optional
3 cups chicken stock (seafood stock or water can be used)
1 cup dry white wine
2½ tablespoons of a gumbo filé
3 bay leaves (mint leaves can also be used)
1½ tablespoons Worcestershire sauce
3 tablespoons parsley, fresh (dry can be used)
Salt and cayenne pepper to taste
3 pounds medium shrimp
1 dozen small blue crabs, cleaned and broken in half
Hot, cooked rice

After the roux is made, add the onion, green pepper, and celery to the roux. Cook vegetables until onions are clear. Add garlic, cook 2 minutes. Add okra and stock. Add rest of the ingredients, except shrimp and crabs to the pot. Cook over low heat for 1 hour. Add water as needed. Add shrimp and crabs and cook for 3 to 5 minutes or until shrimp are pink. Serve over rice.

*Note:* Never add hot water or stock to hot roux. The roux will separate.

*Makes 10 to 12 servings.*

## Keyshala's Gumbo
*Keyshala Waggoner*

1 bunch each mustard and collard greens
1 bunch turnips
1 bunch watercress
1 bunch each beet and carrot tops
½ head lettuce
½ head cabbage
1 bunch spinach
2 medium onions, chopped
4 cloves garlic, mashed and chopped
Water
1 pound each smoked sausage and ham
1 pound chaurice (hot, Cajun-smoked sausage)
2 pounds boneless brisket stew meat
5 tablespoons all-purpose flour
1 teaspoon thyme leaves
1 teaspoon salt
1 teaspoon cayenne pepper
1 teaspoon filé powder
Hot, cooked rice

Clean all vegetables carefully. In a large pot, place all greens, onions, and garlic. Cover with water and boil for 30 minutes. Cut all meats into bite-size pieces and set aside. Strain vegetables and reserve liquid. In a 12-quart stockpot, place brisket, ham, smoked sausage, and 2 cups reserved liquid. Steam for 15 minutes. While steaming place chaurice in a bowl; set aside, keeping the grease in the skillet and set aside. All vegetables must be pureed in a food processor or a meat grinder. Heat skillet or chaurice grease and stir in flour (this becomes the roux for the gumbo). Cook roux for 5 minutes or until flour is cooked (does not have to be brown). Pour roux over meat mixture; stir well. Add vegetables and 2 quarts reserved liquid. Simmer for 20 minutes, add chaurice, thyme, salt, and cayenne pepper; stir well. Simmer for 40 minutes. Add filé powder; stir well and remove from heat.

*Makes 8 servings.*

# SALADS

In Tennessee so many fresh garden vegetables are available that a creative cook can present a veritable showcase of salads. From the simple, traditional cole slaw to hot chicken salad to a grand tossed salad, these delicacies will precede any entrée with mouth-watering delight.

Vegetable gardens, where you gather lettuce, tomatoes, carrots, onions and other salad favorites, have a long history in Middle Tennessee. From tiny plots in the backyards of houses on Main Street to large truck gardens on the properties of places like the beautiful Cullum Mansion in its heydey, Middle Tennesseans just have to grow things. And what they grow, they eat.

# The Cullum Mansion

Using slave labor and hand-fired brick, William Cullum built this home in 1848 in the heart of what is now Carthage.

A cluster of Doric columns on the front entrance of this Greek Revival-style home emphasizes the simple, bold design of this hilltop beauty.

The elegant spiral staircase in the foyer of the mansion is said to have been originally intended for Andrew Jackson's famous Hermitage house. And almost every room has a still-functional marble-and-granite fireplace with a wooden mantel.

The present owners, Dollie and Jim Cowan, have spent many months in extensive renovation to restore the proud lady to her former grandeur. It was a special day when this great old house was entered into the National Register of Historic Places in 1983.

# Apple Salad
*Mary Marsh*

2 cups unpared apples, diced
½ cup celery, diced
½ cup chopped nuts
¾ cup carrots, shredded
½ cup raisins
½ cup mayonnaise or salad dressing

Combine all ingredients and toss to mix.
*Makes 6 to 8 servings.*

# Cucumber Salad
*Rhonda Rush*

2 large cucumbers, sliced
1 large onion, sliced
1½ cups vinegar
1½ cups cold water
Sugar to taste

Mix all ingredients in large bowl. Chill overnight in refrigerator. Serve cold. This is delicious with any meal.
*Makes 4 to 6 servings.*

# Country Garden Salad

1 pound new potatoes
½ pound fresh green beans
4 green onions or scallions
1 head green lettuce leaves
2 firm ripe tomatoes, sliced
2 cucumbers, sliced
1 pound baby carrots
½ pound celery, sliced
1 cup cooked chickpeas

1 cup cooked kidney beans
Salt
Black pepper
2 tablespoons red wine vinegar
½ cup olive oil
1 tablespoon chopped basil
1 cup chicken salad

Boil potatoes in their jackets. Cool and slice. Trim green beans; cut into 1 to 2-inch lengths. Cook in lightly salted water until crisp and tender. Trim green tops from onions or scallions and slice white stems.

Arrange lettuce on a large serving platter. Place tomatoes around the edge, then add remaining vegetables, except onions, in separate mounds on the platter (any vegetable of your choice may be used).

Dissolve a pinch of salt and pepper in vinegar. Add oil and mix thoroughly. Sprinkle with chopped basil and onions. Serve with chilled chicken salad.
*Makes 8 to 10 servings.*

# Zesty Potato Salad
*Nancy Henry*

4 medium potatoes
1 purple onion, diced
3 stalks celery, diced
1 cup zesty Italian salad dressing

Wash and peel potatoes. Cut potatoes into chunks and cook in boiling water until tender. In a large bowl, combine potatoes, onion, and celery. Add Italian salad dressing. Mix all ingredients together. Refrigerate for 2 to 3 hours before serving.
*Makes 4 servings.*

# The Amazing Clinton-Gore Store

The Clinton-Gore Store is a *must stop* when you come to Carthage. Whether you are an Al Gore fan or not, you have to see this store to believe it. When you enter the door, life-sized figures of Bill Clinton and Al Gore Jr. are waving hello. That may startle you into a sharp right turn where George Bush Sr. is sticking his hand out to welcome you.

If those aren't enough greetings from the politically correct, turn back to your left and you will see President Clinton as a long-haired hippie guitar player teamed up with himself on saxophone.

Spread out on counters everywhere are campaign buttons, political pins, patriotic flags and Gore memorabilia from the past twenty years. Postcards, pictures, pens—

you name it, and Bill Markham has stocked it in the Markham Department Store. Of course he carries more traditional items, too, like socks, shoes and gloves, but it's more fun to browse through the colorful array of paraphernalia than to shop for those ordinary items.

One store clerk says she is getting a kick out of all the tourists coming in. "They all have questions about the Gores and the history behind some of these pieces," she says. The store is always prepared for whatever political campaign is coming up next with cases of campaign-slogan buttons and pins. "Things can get really busy right quick around here, and 2000 will be fun."

*Bill Markham, who created The Clinton-Gore Store*

# Red Potato Salad

8 to 10 large red potatoes (about 4 pounds)
½ sweet red pepper, cut into thin strips
Watercress Mayonnaise (recipe follows)
Watercress
Tomato wedges

Cook potatoes in boiling water to cover 30 minutes or until tender. Drain and cool slightly. Cut into chunks. Combine potatoes and red pepper in a large bowl; stir in Watercress Mayonnaise. Place on a bed of watercress and arrange tomato wedges around salad.

**Watercress Mayonnaise**
1½ cups mayonnaise
½ cup watercress leaves, chopped
1 tablespoon chopped fresh dill
½ teaspoon salt
⅛ teaspoon ground white pepper
1 teaspoon chives
Combine all ingredients in a food processor or electric blender; process until smooth.
*Makes about 1½ cups.*

*Makes about 9 cups when combined.*

# Traditional Potato Salad
*Margaret Stone*

3 medium potatoes
1 tablespoon cider vinegar

1 teaspoon sugar
½ cup celery, chopped
⅓ cup onion, chopped
¼ cup olives, chopped
½ teaspoon salt
½ teaspoon celery seed
¾ cup mayonnaise
2 hard-boiled eggs, chopped

In saucepan, cook potatoes in boiling water until tender. Peel and cube. Place in medium bowl. Sprinkle with vinegar and sugar. Add celery, onion, olives, salt, and celery seed. Fold in mayonnaise and eggs. Cover and refrigerate for 1 hour.
*Makes 4 servings.*

# Ranch Cheese Potato Salad
*Marsha Riddle*

8 large red potatoes
1 package ranch salad dressing mix
1½ cups mayonnaise
¼ cup milk
½ cup Colby cheese, cubed
½ cup Monterey Jack cheese, cubed
¼ cup bacon bits

Cook potatoes in boiling water until tender. Drain and cut into chunks. In a large bowl, stir ranch dressing mix, mayonnaise, and milk.
*(Ranch Cheese Potato Salad, cont'd)*
Add potatoes, Colby, and Monterey Jack cheeses. Stir gently. Sprinkle bacon bits on top and chill.
*Makes 8 servings.*

# Apple Chicken Salad

1 medium apple, cored and chopped
1 cup diced, cooked chicken
2 to 4 tablespoons regular or light
  mayonnaise
2 tablespoons green pepper, diced
1 teaspoon pimiento, chopped
Dash of dried rosemary, crushed
Dash of lemon pepper
Lettuce leaf
Alfafa sprouts, optional

In a small bowl, combine first 7 ingredients. Chill until ready to serve. Place lettuce leaf on a serving plate and top with the chilled chicken salad. Garnish with alfalfa sprouts, if desired.
*Makes 1 serving.*

# Layered Salad

4 cups torn Bibb lettuce
4 cups torn iceberg lettuce
6 large hard-boiled eggs, sliced
1 cup celery, chopped
1 cup green onions, sliced
1 pound bacon, cooked and crumbled
1 8-ounce can sliced water chestnuts, drained
1 10-ounce package frozen English peas,
  thawed
1½ to 2 cups mayonnaise or salad dressing
½ cup Parmesan cheese, grated
2 tablespoons sugar
Pepper rings
Fresh parsley sprigs

Layer first 8 ingredients in a large bowl. Combine mayonnaise and next 2 ingredients; spread over peas, sealing to edge of bowl. Cover and refrigerate 8 hours or overnight. Garnish with pepper rings and parsley sprigs.
*Makes 8 to 10 servings.*

# Joseph's Hot Chicken Salad
*Joseph Law*

3 cups chopped chicken or turkey
2 10¾-ounce cans cream of chicken soup
3 cups onion, chopped
Pepper to taste
½ teaspoon salt
1 cup mayonnaise
6 hard-boiled eggs, chopped
2 teaspoons lemon juice
1 cup cracker crumbs
1 cup almonds, slivered
Chow mein noodles or shredded cheese

Preheat oven to 350°. Mix first 10 ingredients together, except noodles or cheese. Top with noodles or cheese. Bake for 30 minutes or until bubbly hot.
*Makes 6 servings.*

# Taco Salad
*Alecia M. Spigner*

1 pound ground beef
1 medium onion, diced
1 package taco seasoning mix
1 16-ounce can hot chili beans
1 medium jar hot taco sauce
1 large bag corn chips
8 ounces sour cream
½ head lettuce, shredded
1 medium tomato, diced
½ cup grated cheese

Brown beef and onion; drain. Stir in taco seasoning, chili beans, and hot sauce. Layer into a 9x13-inch casserole dish with half the corn chips. Place meat mixture on top. Layer sour cream, lettuce, tomato, and cheese. Top with remaining crushed corn chips.
*Makes 4 to 6 servings.*

*Carthage residents are not modest about their support for the hometown candidate for President, Al Gore Jr.*

# Cheese and Walnut Salad
*Andrea Stewart-Waggoner*

1 small head romaine lettuce
1 bunch celery hearts, julienned
¾ cup shelled walnuts, chopped coarse
¼ pound semi-soft cheese
2 ounces bleu cheese
½ cup vegetable oil
Salt and pepper
2 hard-boiled eggs, sliced

Rinse lettuce, dry thoroughly, and tear the leave into pieces. Place in salad bowl. Add celery and chopped walnuts. Dice cheeses and add to the salad bowl. Pour oil very slowly over salad and season to taste with salt and pepper. Toss gently. Garnish with egg slices to serve.

*Makes 4 servings.*

# Tarragon-Shrimp and Orange Rice Salad
*Andrea Stewart-Waggoner*

1 cup long-grain rice (uncooked)
1 pound fresh asparagus
1 pound unpeeled medium-size fresh shrimp
2 slices bacon, cut into ½ inch pieces
1 shallot, chopped
1 tablespoon olive oil
¾ cup mayonnaise
¼ cup green onions, sliced
1 tablespoon chopped fresh tarragon
1 teaspoon capers
¼ teaspoon salt
⅛ teaspoon freshly ground pepper
2 teaspoons grated orange rind
2 oranges, peeled and sectioned
Fresh tarragon
Asparagus tips
Orange sections

Cook rice according to package directions; cool. Set aside. Snap off tough ends of asparagus. Remove scales from stalks with a knife or vegetable peeler, if desired. Arrange asparagus in a vegetable steamer over boiling water; cover and steam for 5 to 7 minutes or until crisp-tender. Let cool and cut into 1½-inch pieces. Set aside.

Peel and de-vein shrimp. Cook shrimp, bacon, and shallot in olive oil in a large skillet over medium-high heat, stirring constantly, for 5 to 7 minutes or until shrimp turns pink. Drain.

Combine mayonnaise and next 6 ingredients in a large bowl; add orange sections, rice, asparagus, and shrimp mixture, tossing gently. Cover and chill. Garnish with tarragon, asparagus tips, and orange sections, if desired.

*Makes 6 servings.*

*Down the road from the Gores' home is Forks River School in Elmwood where they vote in political elections.*

*Vice President Al Gore and his daughter, Kristen, wait their turn as Tipper signs in to vote.*

When he was still alive Al Gore Sr. also voted at the Forks River School.

*Al Gore Jr. signs the voting register.*

## Macaroni Salad
*Marsha Riddle*

1 8-ounce package macaroni
¼ cup mayonnaise
½ cup sour cream
2 tablespoons onion, grated
3 tablespoons parsley
1 cup ripe olives, sliced
1 tablespoon pimiento, diced
1 tablespoon vinegar
1 teaspoon garlic powder
2 hard-boiled eggs, sliced

Cook macaroni in boiling water. Rinse in cold water and drain. In large bowl, mix macaroni and all remaining ingredients together. Chill and serve.
*Makes 4 servings.*

## Spaghetti Salad
*Regina Dickens Brooks*

1 8-ounce box thin spaghetti
2 tomatoes
2 cucumbers
1 green pepper
1 bunch green onions, optional
½ bottle Salad Supreme
   (found in area with seasonings and salt)
1 package dry Italian Dressing mix
1 16-ounce bottle Zesty Italian dressing
Salt and pepper to taste

Prepare spaghetti as directed on box. Drain and set aside to cool. While spaghetti is cooling, cut the vegetables into large cubes and mix together. Shake Salad Supreme over cooled spaghetti and toss.

Pour dry dressing mix into bottled dressing and shake to mix thoroughly. Toss vegetables in with spaghetti, then pour on dressing mixture. Toss well. Season with salt and pepper to taste. Cover tightly and refrigerate overnight.
*Makes 4 to 6 servings.*

## Freezer Slaw
*Mrs. Grady L. (Willa) York*

1 large head cabbage, chopped or grated
   (about 6 cups)
1 large onion, chopped
Salt
1 cup sugar
1 cup vinegar
⅔ cup vegetable oil
½ cup sweet pepper, chopped
1 cup carrots, chopped
1 tablespoon salt
1 teaspoon celery seed
1 teaspoon mustard seed

Combine chopped vegetables; sprinkle with salt and sugar. Let stand about 15 minutes. Combine remaining ingredients and bring to a boil. Pour over cabbage mixture, mixing ingredients well. Place in airtight containers to freeze. Thaw and eat as desired.
*Makes 8 to 10 servings.*

# Mrs. Gore's Spiced Cole Slaw

*Pauline Gore*

1 medium cabbage
3 green peppers
3 onions
1 cup sugar
Salt and black pepper to taste
Vinegar

Use food processor to grind cabbage, peppers, and onions. Mix with sugar, salt, and pepper. Mix enough vinegar, diluted with a little water, to yield desired consistency. Mrs. Gore says she uses 2 cups vinegar and ¼ cup water. (Add some vinegar and sugar; cook about 30 to 40 minutes to make an excellent relish.)

*Makes 6 to 8 servings.*

# Crunchy Cole Slaw

*Wilma Fisher*

1 16-ounce package coleslaw mix
2 packages Ramen chicken-flavored noodles
3 green onions, chopped
1 6-ounce package slivered almonds
1 6-ounce package sunflower seeds

Mix first 5 ingredients, place in refrigerator. Chill for 1-2 hours.

**Dressing**
2 packages Ramen chicken-flavored seasoning
½ cup sugar
½ cup cider vinegar
½ cup vegetable oil

Mix remaining ingredients together vigorously. After salad mixture is chilled, pour dressing mixture over it and stir well.

*Makes 6 to 8 servings.*

*The Rotary Club's annual pancake breakfast.*

## Apple Walnut Slaw
*Martha Taylor*

1 16-ounce bag of coleslaw
¾ cup chopped walnuts
½ cup light mayonnaise
½ cup buttermilk
½ cup dark raisins
¼ cup minced onion
2 tablespoons sugar
1 tablespoon lemon juice
½ teaspoon salt
¼ teaspoon pepper
2 apples, cored, and cut into wedges

In large bowl, mix all ingredients, except apples. Gently fold in apples, being careful not to break them. Refrigerate for 2 hours before serving.
*Makes 6 to 8 servings.*

## Baked Potato Dressing
*Cathy Kemp*

1 6-ounce can evaporated milk, chilled
1 8-ounce package cream cheese, softened to room temperature
2 cups mayonnaise (not salad dressing)
2 teaspoons garlic salt

In small mixing bowl, beat milk until fluffy. Add remaining ingredients and beat until well blended. This dressing is great on baked potatoes, salads, vegetables, meats, etc. It stores well for 2 to 3 weeks in the refrigerator, but probably won't last that long. Delicious!
*Makes about 3½ cups.*

## Tennessee Lime Salad
*Lucy Hackett Oldham*

1 3-ounce package lime gelatin
1 8-ounce can crushed pineapple
2 tablespoons sugar
1 cup whipping cream, whipped or substitute
2 cups whipped topping.
  (If whipped topping is used, use only 1 tablespoon of sugar.)
1 cup cottage cheese
½ to 1 cup chopped pecans

Mix gelatin, pineapple, and sugar together and boil for 3 minutes. Set aside to cool. May be placed in refrigerator for a short time. Whip cream until soft peaks form and add cottage cheese and chopped pecans. Mix with the cooled pineapple mixture. (It is best to mix slowly; pour this mixture into the whipped cream or whipped topping mixture.) Pour in small mold or dish and cool in refrigerator until set.
*Makes 4 to 6 servings.*

# Congealed Strawberry Salad
*Sue Bucy*

2 cups boiling water
2 3-ounce boxes strawberry gelatin
1 16-ounce package frozen strawberries
3 bananas
1 8-ounce can crushed pineapple
16 ounces sour cream

Pour boiling water over gelatin; add strawberries. Mash the bananas and add them along with the pineapple. Pour half of the mixture into an oblong mold. Place in refrigerator and allow to congeal. Carefully spread with sour cream and refrigerate again. After sour cream has become thoroughly chilled, top with the remaining gelatin. Refrigerate until firm. May be unmolded or cut into squares.
*Makes 4 to 6 servings.*

# Cherry Cola Salad
*Vickey Key*

1 21-ounce can cherry pie filling
2½ cups water, divided
½ cup sugar
2 3-ounce packages cherry gelatin
1 cup cola
1 20-ounce can crushed pineapple
½ cup chopped pecans

Combine pie filling, ½ cup water and sugar. Bring to a boil for 5 minutes. Set aside to cool. Mix gelatin with 2 cups boiling water. Add cola. Cool until mixture thickens. Mix pineapple and nuts into cherry filling mixture. Chill until firm.
*Makes 6 servings.*

# Pistachio Salad
*Millie Gwaltney*

1 12-ounce container whipped topping
1 3-ounce package pistachio pudding mix
1 20-ounce can crushed pineapple with juice
1 cup mini-marshmallows
1 cup chopped nuts
½ cup cherries
½ cup coconut

Mix all ingredients together and chill about three hours.
*Makes 6 to 8 servings.*

# Evelyn Duncan's Frozen Fruit Salad
*Millie Gwaltney*

1 21-ounce can strawberry or cherry pie filling
1 16-ounce carton whipped topping
1 16-ounce can crushed pineapple
1 14-ounce can Eagle Brand milk
1 cup chopped nuts

Mix all ingredients well. Freeze in cake pan or glass bowl.
*Makes 6 to 8 servings.*

*Democratic congressional candidate Al Gore Jr. in 1976 talks to members of his campaign organization after a campaign strategy picnic lunch at his home near Carthage.*

# Strawberry Glazed Fruit Salad
*Louise Blackburn*

1 quart fresh strawberries, halved
1 20-ounce can pineapple chunks, drained
4 firm bananas, sliced (not too thin)
1 16-ounce jar or pouch strawberry glaze

In a large bowl, gently toss strawberries, pineapple and bananas. Fold in the glaze. Chill for 1 hour.
*Makes 6 to 8 servings.*

# Aunt Floy's White Christmas Salad
*Millie Gwaltney*

2 cups whipping cream
2 7-ounce jars marshmallow crème
1⅓ cups chopped almonds
⅔ cup each: chopped red and green candied cherries
2 8½-ounce cans crushed pineapple, drained
⅓ cup lemon juice
1 teaspoon rum extract
1 teaspoon almond extract

Preheat oven to 400°. Whip cream until stiff. Gradually beat in marshmallow crème. Spread 1 cup almonds in baking pan and toast for about 8 minutes, stirring occasionally. Reserve ⅓ cup almonds for garnish. Fold almonds and cherries into cream mixture, along with pineapple, lemon juice, and extracts. Turn into an 8-cup mold and freeze. Unmold onto plate and garnish with almonds, red and green cherries.
*Makes 4 to 6 servings.*

# Orange Delight Salad
*Glyn Sue Collins*

1 6-ounce box vanilla instant pudding
3 tablespoons instant orange drink mix
1 20-ounce can pineapple chunks
1 16-ounce can sliced peaches
1 cup mandarin oranges
4 to 5 bananas, sliced

Mix pudding mix and drink mix together. Drain pineapple juice into mixture. May use peach juice if more juice is needed. Add oranges, pineapple chunks, peaches, and bananas; mix well. Chill overnight or several hours.
*Makes 6 to 8 servings.*

## Cranberry Relish
*Christy Scudder*

1 16-ounce can cranberry sauce
  (whole cranberries)
1 large orange, peeled and chopped
2 large firm red apples, chopped
1 16-ounce can crushed pineapple, drained
1 cup chopped pecans
¾ to 1 cup sugar (or to desired sweetness)

Mix all ingredients together two days ahead of time. Keep refrigerated.
*Makes about 6 cups.*

## Cucumber Relish
*Leanne Hesson*

3 cups sugar
2 cups vinegar
8 cups cucumber, minced
2 cups onion, chopped
2 whole sweet peppers, ground
2 tablespoons salt
2 teaspoons celery seed
1 teaspoon tumeric

Bring sugar and vinegar to boil on stove. Add remaining ingredients. Simmer for 20 minutes. Seal in hot, clean glass jars. Excellent with pinto beans!
*Makes about 6 pints.*

# Main Dishes

The main dishes featured here include the traditional Sunday favorites, as well as various ethnic dishes, and some tasty new ways to prepare old standbys. Most of these dishes include meat, whether it's chicken breasts, a casserole, a baked meat, or a crockpot full of meat and vegetables.

Still, there is nothing better than a good old hamburger with all the trimmings, like the ones you can get at the B & B Drive-In. And if you come to try them out, be sure to bring your appetite.

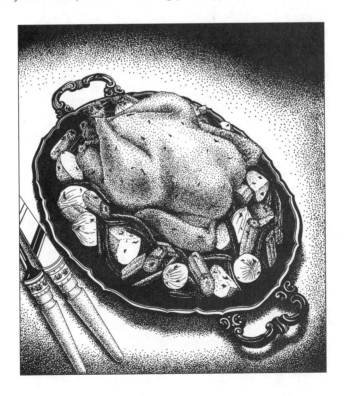

# B & B Drive-In Restaurant

When it comes to eating out, a favorite hang-out is the B & B Drive-In. Just sit at a table in Miss Bonnie's cafe for an hour or so, and you will soon find out what's really going on around town. The "regulars" come in, have a cup of coffee, and talk about the day's happenings. If you listen closely, you'll soon be up to date. Pickup trucks and high-tech sports cars sit side by side out front just off the road that runs east from Al Gore's house.

Overalled farmers, suited business people, and teens sit elbow-to-elbow in the B & B. The smell of fried foods and hot bread fills the air. Friendly hellos. Familiar faces. And time . . . time to sit and talk and think.

Miss Bonnie Kinney, the owner of the thirty-two-year-old restaurant, says that Al Gore Jr. ate there almost every night during the summers he spent as a teenager on the family farm outside of Carthage.

"His favorite food was hamburgers," says Bonnie, whose restaurant is now run by her son. "I guess he could eat a hamburger every night."

The B & B Drive-In is much the same today as it was during Al Jr.'s teen days. And its specialty still remains double-handed, thick 'n' juicy hamburgers. Some things never change. Some things never should!

# Low-Calorie Classic Chicken
*Gladys Gibbs*

3 slices bacon
1 16-ounce package frozen cauliflower florets
3 tablespoons butter
4 tablespoons all-purpose flour
Dash of white pepper
1½ cups chicken broth
½ cup low-fat milk
⅔ cup cream of chicken soup
½ cup low-fat buttermilk
2 tablespoons low-fat yogurt
2 tablespoons reduced-fat sour cream
1 teaspoon lemon juice
2 cups cooked chicken, cubed
4 ounces shredded low-moisture part-skim
    mozzarella cheese
1 cup soft bread crumbs
2 tablespoons butter, melted
1 tablespoon grated Parmesan cheese

Cook bacon until crisp; crumble and set aside. Cook cauliflower according to package directions; drain. Melt butter in double boiler over boiling water; blend in flour and dash of pepper. Add chicken broth and low-fat milk; cook and stir until mixture thickens. Stir in cream of chicken soup. Remove from heat; add buttermilk, yogurt, sour cream, and lemon juice. Preheat oven to 350°.

Place cauliflower in 2-quart round or 8x8-inch square baking dish. Pour half the sauce over cauliflower. Add crumbled bacon and top with chicken. To remaining sauce, add mozzarella cheese and pour over chicken. Set aside.

Mix bread crumbs with melted butter. Add Parmesan cheese; mix well. Sprinkle around edge of cauliflower and chicken. Bake for 20 minutes, then broil until crumb topping is golden (about 4 minutes).
*Makes 6 servings.*

# Baked Chicken Breasts Supreme
*Martha Taylor*

1½ cups plain, low-fat yogurt
¼ cup lemon juice
½ teaspoon Worcestershire sauce
½ teaspoon celery seed
½ teaspoon paprika
1 clove garlic, minced
¼ teaspoon white pepper
8 boneless chicken breasts
2 cups fine dry bread crumbs

In a large mixing bowl, combine first seven ingredients. Place chicken in mixture and turn to coat. Cover and marinate in the refrigerator for at least 1 hour. Preheat oven to 350°. Remove chicken from marinade. Coat each piece with bread crumbs. Arrange on ungreased baking pan. Bake, uncovered, for 45 minutes.
*Makes 8 servings.*

## Farmer in the Dell
*Mattie Payne*

Mrs. Mattie Payne was kind enough to share a popular recipe for Farmer in the Dell.

Before many of Mr. and Mrs. Gore's cattle sales there would be an annual pre-sale dinner on the Gore farm. Farmer in the Dell was one dish prepared by Mrs. Gore and Mattie for the occasion.

1 5-pound chicken, stewed
Flour
2 sticks butter
Salt and pepper to taste
1 20-ounce can tomatoes, chopped
3 onions, chopped
3 green peppers, chopped
1 small bunch celery, chopped
¼ pound currants
1½ teaspoons curry
¼ pound almonds

Dice chicken, roll in flour, salt and pepper, and brown in butter. Combine next 5 ingredients and cook together until tender. Mix chicken and vegetable mixture. Cook until heated throughout. Add the almonds last. Serve while hot.
*Makes 10 to 12 servings.*

## Molly's Famous Fried Chicken
*Molly M. Bowman*

1 cup milk
1 egg, beaten
Dash of garlic powder or salt
Salt and pepper to taste
Flour
Chicken pieces
Vegetable oil

Mix milk, egg, garlic powder, salt, and pepper. Dip chicken pieces in mixture; roll in flour. Fry on medium heat. *Hint:* For best results, soak chicken in cold salt water for at least 2 hours before frying.
*Makes 4 to 6 servings.*

## Fried Chicken Gravy

6 to 8 tablespoons strained oil from frying
½ cup all-purpose flour
Salt, optional
2 to 3 cups water or milk
Brown gravy coloring, optional

Strain oil from chicken frying skillet, leaving crispy bits in skillet; add any reserved bits. Return 6 to 8 tablespoons oil to skillet. Add flour and salt to skillet; blend well over medium heat. Brown flour-fat mixture, stirring constantly. Stir in water or milk. (Milk will produce a creamier gravy.) Cook, stirring constantly, until gravy thickens. If not brown enough, add a little gravy coloring.
*Makes 2 to 3 cups.*

*In 1974* Tennessean *reporter Al Gore initiated a probe in which a Nashville councilman was indicted on bribery charges. Here the young reporter confers with chief photographer Bill Preston.*

# Sesame Chicken

2 large, split chicken breasts*
½ stick butter, melted
2 tablespoons grated Parmesan cheese
¼ teaspoon salt
⅛ teaspoon crumbled, dried thyme
⅛ teaspoon pepper
1 tablespoon sesame seed

Preheat oven to broil. Rinse and thoroughly dry chicken breasts. Place skin-side up in center of a sheet of foil. Combine melted butter, Parmesan cheese, salt, pepper, and thyme. Spoon about ½ of mixture over chicken. Fold foil over chicken and seal. Place on broiler pan; slip under broiler, about 4 inches from heat, for 20 to 25 minutes (*Optional:* Put in a 350° oven and bake for about 30 minutes.)

Unfold foil; fold down, forming it into a shallow pan with edges. Add sesame seed to remaining butter mixture. Spread a spoonful of the sesame mixture on top of each breast. Return to broiler for 3 to 5 minutes or until sesame seeds are browned.

Pour juices into a bowl for gravy. Delicious over white rice. This is nice for guests because this recipe can be prepared and sealed in the foil early in the day, then placed in the oven at the proper time.

*Choose large chicken breasts; each split chicken breast should weigh almost ½ pound.
*Makes 2 servings.*

# Chicken and Biscuits

1 (2½– to 3–pound) frying chicken, cut up
½ cup all-purpose flour
½ cup wheat germ
1½ teaspoons paprika
2 teaspoons salt
1 stick butter or margarine
Biscuit mix
⅓ cup wheat germ

Preheat oven to 425°. Dip chicken pieces in mixture of flour, ½ cup wheat germ, paprika, and salt. Coat well. Melt butter or margarine in shallow baking dish (9x13x2 inches) in a hot oven. Remove baking dish from oven and place chicken skin-side down in a single layer. Bake for 45 minutes. Turn chicken.

Prepare your favorite packaged biscuit mix according to directions on package. Enrich it by adding ⅓ cup wheat germ to the dry mix. Add milk called for in directions plus 1 extra tablespoon. Roll dough; cut biscuits.

Place in one end of baking pan, pushing chicken to other end. Be sure both chicken and biscuits remain in single layer. Bake another 15 minutes or until biscuits are lightly browned.
*Makes 4 servings.*

# Dixona

Come on by and rest on the verandah at Dixona. Sit in the sweet sunshine, admire the profusion of flowers, and let Faith Young enthrall you with stories of the old days. You will never want to leave. Guaranteed. Throw in Faith's sweet-and-tangy lemonade, and life slows to a bearable pace.

"The rural living style of the South is really here," says Faith. Sip your lemonade, listen to the wicker rocker squeak, and enjoy the gentle breeze on your face.

In 1788 Tilman Dixon of North Carolina built this magnificent log house on his 3,840-acre estate. You can still see the giant logs that line the verandah. Dixona, as it was called, became a favorite stopping place for Dixon's friends, who preferred more genteel surroundings that included coffee and good food. This frontier home also served as a courthouse and tavern.

The furnishings and reproductions are true to the list on file at the Smith County Courthouse. High beds are still made exactly as they were two hundred years ago; diaries written and signed in the late 1700s are lying about; clothes hang on the walls as if left there two hours ago rather than two centuries ago. Antique books and furniture are decorated with Indian artifacts.

Faith and "Billy," as she likes to call her husband, host a 45-year-old annual Deer Hunters' Dinner in the style of the eighteenth century gentlemen hunters. People come from all over Middle Tennessee for it. The men do all the

cooking of wild game and venison. They even make hominy from real ashes in the fireplace.

When Faith talks about Dixona and Carthage, she says sadly, "Progress is the problem. We know we have to move forward, but what we leave behind are places like this, places where we can slow down, contemplate, and just visit."

Dixona, the oldest house in Middle Tennessee, is a place to enjoy a rare privilege described in this old saying: "Sometimes I sits and thinks, and sometimes I just sits."

*Historic Dixona*

# Faith Young's Barbeque Sauce

2 cups onions
4 cloves garlic
1 cup oil
4 cups catsup
1 cup brown sugar
1 cup Worcestershire sauce

8 tablespoons mustard (prepared)
4 teaspoons salt
1 teaspoon thyme
4 thinly sliced lemons
4 dashes hot sauce

Stir together and keep in refrigerator indefinitely. Good on venison, chicken, and wild game.

# Country Chicken and Dumplings

1 3- to 3½-pound broiler-fryer
2 quarts water
2 stalks celery, cut into pieces
1 teaspoon salt
2 cups all-purpose flour
2 teaspoons baking powder
½ to ¾ teaspoon salt
1 stick butter or margarine, softened to room temperature

Place chicken in a Dutch oven; add water, celery, and 1 teaspoon salt. Bring to a boil; cover, reduce heat, and simmer 1 hour or until tender. Remove chicken from broth and cool. Discard celery. Debone chicken and cut meat into bite-size pieces; set aside meat and ¾ cup broth. Bring remaining broth to a boil.

Combine flour, baking powder, and ½ teaspoon salt; cut in butter until mixture resembles coarse meal. Add ¾ cup reserved broth, stirring with a fork until dry ingredients are moistened. Turn dough out onto a well-floured surface and knead.

Pat dough to a ½-inch thickness. Cut dough into 4 x ½-inch pieces and sprinkle with additional flour. Drop dough, one piece at a time, into boiling broth, gently stirring after each addition. Reduce heat to low; cover and cook for 8 to 10 minutes. Stir in chicken and serve immediately.

*Makes 4 servings.*

# Cheesy Chicken Crescent Dinner

*Peggy Chapman*

1 10¾-ounce can creamy chicken-mushroom soup
1 cup milk
1 cup shredded Cheddar cheese, divided
1 8-ounce can crescent rolls
1¾ cups cubed, cooked chicken

Preheat oven to 375°. Combine soup, milk, and ⅓ cup cheese in a medium saucepan. Heat on low until cheese melts. Separate rolls; on the wide end of each roll put several pieces of chicken. Cover with half the cheese. Roll up. Pour half of soup mixture into oblong glass casserole. Arrange crescents into dish. Bake for 20 to 25 minutes or until crescent rolls are brown. Sprinkle with remaining cheese and return to oven until melted. Cover with remaining sauce.

*Makes 4 to 6 servings.*

## Chicken Pot Pie

*Susie George*

2 16-ounce cans mixed vegetables
2 10¾-ounce cans cream of chicken soup
1 8-ounce can mushrooms, drained
2 skinless cooked chicken breasts.
Frozen pie dough for top and bottom crust

Preheat oven to 350°. In a large bowl, combine mixed vegetables, soup, and mushrooms. Cut chicken into small pieces, and add to mixture in bowl. Stir well. Pour into pie shell. Add top crust. Bake for 1 hour or until golden brown.
*Makes 4 servings.*

## Hearty Pot Pies

1 13-ounce can solid white tuna or chicken
1 pound boiling potatoes unpared, cut into chunks
½ pound carrots, cut in ¼-inch slices
3 stalks celery, cut in 2-inch pieces
1 clove garlic, pressed
1 small onion, chopped
½ teaspoon thyme, crumbled
¼ teaspoon pepper
3 tablespoons butter or margarine
3 tablespoons all-purpose flour
2½ cups chicken broth
2 egg yolks
1 cup frozen peas
Corn Meal Crust (recipe follows)

Drain tuna/chicken. In large saucepan, boil potatoes, carrots, and celery 7 minutes. Drain. In large skillet, sauté garlic, onion, thyme, and pepper in butter. Blend in flour. Stir in chicken broth until mixture thickens. Remove from heat. Beat in egg yolks. Add tuna/chicken, cooked vegetables, and peas. Spoon into 4 2-cup individual casserole dishes. Top with Corn Meal Crust. Bake in 375° oven 25 to 30 minutes. Cool 5 minutes before serving.

**Corn Meal Crust**
1 stick butter or margarine, softened to room temperature
⅓ cup corn meal
2 eggs
1¼ cup all-purpose flour
2 teaspoons baking powder

In medium bowl, beat butter with corn meal. Add eggs, one at a time, until blended. Beat in flour and baking powder. Knead for 1 minute. Divide into 4 pieces. Shape to fit over pot pies.
*Makes 4 servings.*

## Chicken & Rice

*Frances Lankford*

½ cup fresh mushrooms, sliced
1 small onion, diced
1 cup chicken pieces
½ cup chicken broth
1 cup instant rice
½ cup cooked carrots
Salt and pepper to taste

Combine fresh mushrooms, onions, chicken, and broth. Cook until chicken is tender. Add remaining ingredients. Cook on medium heat for another 30 minutes. This is a very good soup mixture.
*Makes 2 servings.*

*In Carthage there are plenty of opportunities to hear great music and dance your shoes off, just as these folks are doing at a local social event.*

## Skillet Broccoli & Chicken
*Helen Shepherd*

1 6½-ounce package chicken-flavored rice-vermicelli mix
2 tablespoons margarine or butter
2 cups water
1 teaspoon dried basil
4 boneless, skinless chicken breast halves
2 cups broccoli florets
1 tomato, chopped
1 cup shredded mozzarella cheese

Sauté rice-vermicelli mix with margarine in large skillet over medium heat until vermicelli is brown. Add water, seasoning packet, and basil. Bring to a boil over high heat. Place chicken breasts on rice. Cover and reduce heat to low. Simmer for about 10 minutes or until chicken is thoroughly cooked. Sprinkle with cheese. Cover and let stand another 3 to 4 minutes to allow cheese to melt.
*Makes 4 servings.*

## Sour Cream Chicken
*Jackson Stewart and Bridgett England*

4 to 5 pieces of chicken
5 slices bacon
1 10¾-ounce can cream of mushroom soup
8 ounces sour cream
Hot, cooked rice

Preheat oven to 425°. Rinse chicken and pat it dry. Wrap bacon around chicken. Place in casserole dish. In a separate bowl, mix soup and sour cream. Pour over chicken. Cover with foil. Bake for 45 minutes or until chicken is tender. Serve over rice.
*Makes 4 servings.*

## Gourmet Chicken
*Mary Leslie Wakefield*

2 10¾-ounce cans cream of chicken soup
1 6-ounce package thin sliced beef
6 to 8 boneless, skinless chicken breasts
Salt and pepper to taste
8 ounces sour cream
Hot, cooked rice

Preheat oven to 350°. Spread ½ can soup on bottom of casserole dish. Layer beef, then chicken breast and salt and pepper. Mix 1 can soup with sour cream. Pour on top of chicken. Cover with foil and bake for 1½ hours or until chicken is tender. Serve with rice.
*Makes 6 to 8 servings.*

## Chicken Divine
*April Denise Shrum*

1 10¾-ounce can cream of chicken soup
1 4-ounce package Cheddar cheese, divided
1 can crescent rolls
3 chicken breasts, cooked and shredded
1 cup milk

Preheat oven to 375°. Heat soup, 2 tablespoons cheese, and milk on low heat until mixed well. Roll up shredded cheese and chicken in crescent rolls. Place into greased casserole and pour soup mixture over top. Bake for 20 to 25 minutes or until golden brown.
*Makes 3 servings.*

*The current home of Al and Tipper Gore outside of Carthage near Elmwood.*

*Mrs. Pauline Gore, recipient of the Community Foundation of Middle Tennessee's 1998 Joe Kraft Humanitarian Award. An attorney in her own right, she was the wife of the late Al Gore Sr. and she is mother of Al Gore Jr. Mrs. Gore remains active in the Carthage community.*

# Chicken Enchilada Casserole
*Sue Bucy*

1 14-ounce can chunk chicken
1 10¾-ounce can cream of chicken soup
1 10¾-ounce can cream of mushroom soup
½ soup can of milk
4 ounces sour cream
1 tablespoon onion flakes
½ 4-ounce can chopped green chilies
8 ounces Cheddar cheese
8 ounces mozzarella cheese
1 8-ounce bag tortilla chips

Preheat oven to 350°. Mix chicken, soups, milk, sour cream, onion, chilies, and ½ of each of the cheeses. Spread ¾ of the chips on bottom of 9x13-inch baking dish. Pour chicken mixture on top of chips. Top with remaining cheeses. Crush remaining chips and sprinkle over top. Bake, covered, for 35 to 40 minutes or until bubbly.
*Makes 4 servings.*

# Kevin's Mexican Chicken Casserole
*Kevin Dickerson*

6 chicken breasts, cooked and de-boned
1 10¾-ounce can cream of chicken soup
1 10¾-ounce can cream of mushroom soup
1 10¾-ounce can Cheddar cheese soup
1 10-ounce can tomatoes with green chilies
1 medium onion, chopped
1 17-ounce bag Doritos

Preheat oven to 350°. Layer chicken in 9x13-inch casserole dish; sprinkle half Doritos over chicken. Mix soups together and heat in microwave, about 1 minute. Pour over chicken pieces. Put tomatoes and chopped onion on top. Bake for about 30 minutes. Sprinkle remaining Doritos on top during the last 10 minutes of baking.
*Makes 6 servings*

# Turkey Lasagna
*Dorothy Hitchcock*

1 pound ground turkey
1 medium onion, chopped
1 26-ounce jar spaghetti sauce
1 box lasagna noodles cooked according to package directions
1 16-ounce carton low-fat cottage cheese
1 12-ounce package shredded mozzarella cheese
Grated Parmesan cheese

Preheat oven to 375°. Brown turkey and chopped onion, add sauce. Drain noodles; coat bottom of pan with sauce, add layer of noodles, cottage cheese, mozzarella cheese, and Parmesan cheese; cover with sauce. Repeat layers. Bake for 30 minutes or until cheese is melted and bubbly.
*Makes 6 to 8 servings.*

*The Press Corps wait outside the Gore property for a glimpse of Al and Tipper. This picture was taken following the Clinton-Gore announcement that they would make a run for the presidency.*

## Grilled Pork Chops
*Beverly Gillispie*

1 stick butter
8 pork chops
Salt
Pepper
Garlic powder

Place pork chops in a deep oblong bowl. Melt butter and add salt, pepper, and garlic powder to taste. Make sure chops are covered well. Take out of bowl and place on a hot grill until done.
*Makes 8 servings.*

## Pepper Pork Chops

6 thick-cut center pork chops
1 8-ounce can tomato sauce
1 7¼-ounce jar roasted red peppers
2 cloves garlic, sliced
½ teaspoon pepper
½ cup corn oil
⅓ cup chopped walnuts
¼ cup grated Parmesan cheese
¼ cup Marsala wine

Preheat oven to 350°. Place chops in 13x9x2-inch baking pan. Bake, turning once, until browned, but not done.

Place remaining ingredients in blender. Whirl until smooth and creamy. Pour over chops and continue baking one hour. Place on platter and garnish with red and green pepper rings.
*Makes 6 servings.*

## 20-Minute Pork Chops
*Frances Baker*

1 tablespoon vegetable oil
4 ½-inch thick pork chops
1 10¾-ounce can condensed creamy onion soup
¼ cup water

Heat oil in skillet. Add chops and cook until browned. Add soup and water. Heat to boiling. Cover and cook over low heat for 5 minutes or until done.
*Makes 4 servings.*

## Pork Chops with Paprika-Dill Sauce

6 ¾-inch thick shoulder pork chops
½ cup all-purpose flour, seasoned with salt and pepper
4 tablespoons butter or margarine
4 medium onions, thinly sliced
2 cloves garlic, minced
2 tablespoons paprika
1 chicken bouillon cube, dissolved in 1 cup boiling water
8 ounces sour cream
2 teaspoons dried dill weed

Dredge chops in seasoned flour (reserve 2 tablespoons). Heat butter in large skillet and brown chops on both sides. Set chops aside.

Add onion and garlic to skillet. Sauté over medium heat until tender, stirring occasionally. Stir in paprika and bouillon. Cook over high heat, scraping pan to release the browned bits that have stuck. Add chops; bring to boiling. Lower heat; cover and simmer for 45 minutes or until chops are tender.

Remove chops to serving dish and keep warm. Blend sour cream and reserved flour; add dill weed. Stir mixture into onion mixture. Cook and stir over medium heat until sauce thickens and is smooth (do not boil). Pour some sauce over chops and serve remainder in heated bowl.
*Makes 6 servings.*

# Opal's Casserole
*Opal Agee*

1 cup shredded, cooked pork
1 cup cooked rice
½ cup onion
½ cup cheese
½ stick butter, melted

Preheat oven to 350°. Mix all ingredients in a casserole dish. Bake for 30 minutes.
*Makes 2 servings.*

# Mrs. Gore's Beef Filet with Madeira Sauce
*Mrs. Pauline Gore*

This is one recipe the Vice President's mother often served for the Gore's cattle sale parties. Anywhere from 200 to 500 guests were served lunch.

6 tablespoons butter, divided
1 5- to 6-pound filet of beef, well trimmed
Salt and freshly ground pepper
Approximately 2 cups Madeira Sauce
    (recipe following)

Preheat oven to 450°. Heat 4 tablespoons butter in a shallow roasting pan. When it is melted, turn the filet until the meat is coated with butter. Sprinkle with salt and pepper. Bake for 25 to 35 minutes, basting frequently. Transfer the meat to a large serving dish and keep warm. Prepare the Madeira sauce in roasting pan. Stir to dissolve the brown particles that cling to the bottom and sides of the pan. Swirl in the remaining 2 tablespoons butter. Slice the filet (slice only the amount to be served immediately, and leave the rest of the filet whole to be sliced later). Spoon the sauce over the beef, or spoon part of it over the beef and serve the rest in a sauceboat.

**Madeira Sauce**
1 tablespoon butter
4 large mushrooms, sliced
⅓ cup Madeira wine
2 tablespoons shallots or onions, finely chopped
Salt and freshly ground pepper
1½ cups brown sauce or 1 10¾-ounce can beef gravy

Heat the butter in a skillet and add the mushrooms, shallots, and wine. Sprinkle with salt and pepper; cook until the shallots are cooked, stirring until most of the liquid evaporates. Add the brown sauce and simmer 15 minutes.

*Makes about 2 cups sauce*
*Makes about 12 servings.*

# The Sweetest Taste This Side of Heaven

Follow your eyes; follow your heart; follow your nose. Tom Stewart did all three in 1974 when he moved his family back to Stewart Hollow just a few miles east of Carthage. But it was his nose that helped him make the final decision to return to the hollow that his daddy had farmed. He remembered the pungent aroma of hams aging in the family smokehouse—the "sweetest taste this side of heaven." When he was a child, Tom and his dad would take a horse and go up in the woods and drag back hickory trees for the smoke-house. Now he usually buys the wood. And like his dad, Tom usually raises and fattens his own pigs: "Just to do it the old way," he says.

To prepare hams for smoking, use a salt cure. When it's done its work, wash the cure off and hang the hams in the smokehouse. Then start the smoke. "The smoke is all important," Tom cautions. He recommends hickory or apple or even sassafras. Mesquite wood is probably the best of all. The hams should be smoked for two weeks and then left hanging until used or they're wrapped. Hams weigh from 45 to 50 pounds and should be one year old or older before using. A perfectly smoked ham can be kept two to three years.

When it's time to prepare the ham for the table, cut the butt ends off and cover the ham with water. Add a half to three-quarters cup of honey or sorghum and let it boil for an hour. The next step is very important. After boiling, remove the ham from the water, wrap it in a newspaper, and then in a blanket. Let it set for twenty-four hours. When you take that wrap off and slice a piece off, it's as tender and done as it can be.

Every year is different in the art of smoking ham. If it's really cold, longer salt cure is needed. If the weather is mild, shorter time is required. One of the oldtime favorite smoking methods was to use corncobs. If Tom had his "druthers," he says he'd probably use corncobs and a little hickory. Tom is teaching his great grandson, Malik Riley, the art of smoking hams, too. Hopefully someday he'll carry on the family tradition.

# Beef Roast with Gravy
*Beverly Gillispie*

1 3– to 4–pound beef roast
1 large onion
2 10¾-ounce cans cream of mushroom soup
1 package Lipton onion soup mix
½ cup water

Place all ingredients in crock pot. Cook on Low overnight. Do not add water that is called for on the soup can.
*Makes 8 to 10 servings.*

# Barbecued Spare Ribs
*Wilma Fisher*

5 to 6 pounds lean spare ribs
⅓ cup tomato sauce
1½ tablespoons Worcestershire sauce
2 tablespoons vinegar
1 teaspoon dry mustard
1 cup water
½ teaspoon chili powder
1 tablespoon sugar
2 medium yellow onions, sliced

Preheat oven to 325°. Cut ribs into serving pieces. Combine remaining ingredients, except onions. Place or layer ribs in baking pan. Place onions over ribs and cover with half the sauce. Repeat layers; cover pan. Bake for 3 hours. Uncover last half hour of cooking time.
*Makes 4 to 6 servings.*

# Barbecue Ribs
*Christy Kemp*

3 to 4 pounds ribs
¾ cup catsup
½ cup vinegar
¾ cup honey
1 teaspoon mustard
Salt and pepper to taste

Boil ribs for 45 minutes. Mix remaining ingredients. Pour over the ribs. Chill overnight. Bake at 350° for 45 minutes.
*Makes 6 to 8 servings.*

# Meat Loaf
*BeLinda Watts*

2 pounds ground beef
1 cup cracker crumbs
½ cup onion, chopped
½ cup sweet pepper, chopped
½ cup celery, chopped
⅛ teaspoon salt
⅛ teaspoon pepper
Dash of sage
Dash of garlic salt
¼ cup milk
1 cup tomato soup

Preheat oven to 350°. Mix all ingredients, except soup, in large bowl and place in a 9x13-inch pan. Cover with soup and bake 1 hour. Remove from oven and let stand about 10 minutes. Drain liquid before serving.
*Makes 8 to 10 servings.*

## Lazy Day Lasagna
*Amanda and Joshua Ragland*

1 pound ground beef
1 26-ounce can spaghetti sauce
Nonstick cooking spray
2 cups cottage cheese
1 8-ounce package mozzarella cheese,
    shredded
8 to 10 lasagna noodles

Brown ground beef. Drain. Add spaghetti sauce to ground beef and set aside. Bring a large pot of water to boil and cook noodles for 5 to 8 minutes. Drain off hot water and cover with cold water. Preheat oven to 350°. Spray a 13x9-inch baking dish with pan spray. Remove noodles from cold water and place 4 to 5 in the baking dish. Place half the cottage cheese on top of noodles. Place mozzarella cheese on top of cottage cheese, spread ½ of sauce mixture on this. Repeat layers and sprinkle with Parmesan cheese if desired. Bake for 20 minutes or until bubbly around edges. Let stand about 10 to 15 minutes before serving.
*Makes 6 to 8 servings.*

## Beefy Onion Casserole
*Glenda Jones*

1 pound ground chuck
1 medium onion, chopped
½ pound shredded Cheddar cheese
1 16-ounce can pork and beans
1 tablespoon barbeque sauce
1 large can biscuits (10)
1 3-ounce can French-fried onions

Preheat oven to 350°. Brown ground chuck, add onion and cook until onions are clear.

Drain and place in a baking dish, add beans, barbecue sauce, and top with cheese. Cut biscuits in half and place around the side of the dish. Place onions in center. Bake for 15 to 20 minutes or until biscuits are browned and cheese is melted.
*Makes 4 to 6 servings.*

## Hayes Hamburger Casserole
*Millie Gwaltney*

1 pound hamburger, browned
2 medium potatoes peeled and chopped
1 medium onion, chopped
1 16-ounce can English peas, drained
1 10¾-ounce can cream of mushroom soup

Preheat oven to 350°. Mix all ingredients together. Pour into casserole dish. Bake for 35 to 40 minutes.
*Makes 4 servings.*

## French Onion Burgers
*Sandra Conder*

1 pound ground beef
1 cup condensed French onion soup (10½-
    ounce can)
4 slices cheese
4 round hard rolls, split

Shape beef into 4 ½-inch thick patties. Cook until done and drain off fat. Add soup to pan. Heat to boiling. Cover and cook over low heat until warmed thoroughly. Top burgers with cheese. Serve rolls with soup mixture for drippings.
*Makes 4 servings.*

*Three generations of the Gore family have thrived on one of the family's favorite recipes—Gore Burgers!*

## Gore Burgers
*Pauline Gore*

1½ pounds ground beef
1½ teaspoons salt
1 medium tomato, finely chopped
1 small cucumber, grated
1 small onion, finely chopped
⅓ cup catsup
⅓ cup sweet pickle relish
8 hamburger buns

Lightly brown ground beef in large frying pan over medium heat; pour off drippings. Sprinkle salt over meat. Add tomato, cucumber, onion, catsup, and relish; stir to combine. Cook, covered, for 15 minutes. Serve on hamburger buns. *Note:* Whole wheat buns or pita pocket bread add a tasty variation.
*Makes 8 servings.*

Tipper Gore is a frequent visitor and speaker at Middle-Tennessee political, educational, and social events. Below she signs an autograph for a young Carthage admirer.

# Cool Weather Chili
### *Sue Thompson*

2 pounds ground beef
1 tablespoon minced onion
½ teaspoon garlic
1 15-ounce can tomato sauce
3 small cans light red kidney beans
1 cup water
1½ teaspoons chili powder

Brown ground beef and drain. Combine all other ingredients and add to beef. Heat until it starts to lightly bubble. Reduce heat. Cover and simmer for 45 minutes, stirring occasionally. Serve hot.
*Makes 4 to 6 servings.*

# Tennessee Chili

2 cups water
1 tablespoon sugar
1 cup beef consommé
2 teaspoons oregano leaves
2 tablespoons paprika
2 tablespoons cumin
1 tablespoon celery salt
1 teaspoon red pepper
7 tablespoons chili powder
1 tablespoon mole paste
1 teaspoon garlic powder
3 tablespoons vegetable oil
2 pounds beef chuck, cut into ⅜-inch cubes
2 pounds top round beef coarsely chopped
2 pounds pork butt, medium ground
2 tablespoons finely minced garlic
1 cup chopped green chilies
1 20-ounce can tomato sauce
1 12-ounce can beer
1 tablespoon masa harina or cornstarch
2 tablespoons water

In a 6-quart stockpot, place water, sugar, consommé, and seasonings; heat and stir until dissolved. Over medium heat, cook until bubbly; cover and continue cooking over low heat.

Meanwhile, cover bottom of large skillet with vegetable oil; heat over medium heat. Add the meats and sauté until lightly browned. Add meat mixture to stockpot. If necessary, add more oil to skillet; sauté onion and garlic until tender but not browned. Add onion mixture to stockpot along with chilies and tomato sauce. Over high heat, bring to boiling. Add beer.

Reduce heat to low and simmer, uncovered, for 1½ to 2 hours, stirring occasionally. Remove from heat and let stand for 30 minutes. Skim off excess grease. Taste and add additional seasonings, if desired. In small bowl, dissolve masa harina in water. Add to chili and stir until thickened. Cover and let stand 1 hour before serving. If a thinner chili is preferred, use less masa harina; for a thicker chili, use more.
*Makes 14 to 16 servings.*

## Cornbread Pie

1 pound ground beef
1 teaspoon sage
1 teaspoon dried basil
¾ teaspoon salt
1 small onion, chopped
1 8-ounce can tomato sauce
1 8-ounce can refried beans
4 ounces mozzarella cheese
⅓ cup corn meal
⅓ cup all-purpose flour
1 teaspoon baking powder
1 teaspoon sugar
⅓ teaspoon salt
3 tablespoons milk
1 egg, slightly beaten
1 tablespoon vegetable oil

Brown beef in a large 10-inch skillet with sage, basil, and ¾ teaspoon salt. Drain well. Stir in onion, tomato sauce, and refried beans. Cook until mixture bubbles. Place beef mixture in 9-inch deep pie pan, pressing to flatten top. Sprinkle cheese over top.

Preheat oven to 350°. For cornbread topping, mix corn meal, flour, baking powder, sugar, and ¼ teaspoon salt in medium bowl. Combine and stir in milk, egg, and oil. Spoon mixture around edge of baking dish. Bake for 25 to 30 minutes. Let stand 3 to 5 minutes before serving.
*Makes 4 servings.*

## Beef Tomato Dinner
*Martha Taylor*

1 pound lean ground beef
2 tablespoons minced onion
1 tablespoon parsley flakes
1 6-ounce can tomato paste
2 cups water
1 teaspoon salt
2 teaspoons chili powder
1 4-ounce can mushrooms, undrained
1 7-ounce package macaroni

Brown beef in skillet; drain any fat. Add onion, parsley flakes, tomato paste, water, salt, chili powder, mushrooms, and macaroni. Bring to a boil. Cover; reduce heat to simmer and cook for about 20 to 25 minutes or until macaroni is tender.
*Makes 6 servings.*

## Barbeque Noodles
*Sally Long*

1 7-ounce bag noodles
1 pound ground beef
1 bell pepper, chopped
1 onion, chopped
1 8-ounce bottle barbeque sauce
8 ounces mozzarella cheese

Boil noodles according to package directions; drain and set aside. Brown ground beef with pepper and onion; drain fat. Add barbeque sauce; heat through. Pour over noodles; stir well. Add cheese, a little at a time, stirring well after each addition. This will be stringy. Serve with salad for a complete meal.
*Makes 4 servings.*

*Al Gore greets senior citizens at a luncheon in Carthage.*

# Meatballs
*Leanne Hesson*

1½ pounds ground beef
¾ cup oats
½ teaspoon salt
½ teaspoon pepper
1 cup milk
4 tablespoons onions, chopped
1 cup catsup
2 tablespoons white vinegar
3 tablespoons brown sugar
½ cup water

Preheat oven to 325°. Combine first six ingredients and form into balls. Place in baking dish. Combine remaining ingredients and pour over meatballs. Bake for 1 hour.
*Makes 6 to 8 servings.*

# Shenia's Sausage Casserole
*Debbie Bush Rich*

2 packages crescent rolls
1 pound bulk pork sausage
1 8-ounce jar Cheez Whiz
1 egg

Preheat oven to 350°. Brown sausage and drain. Beat Cheez Whiz, egg, and sausage together. Butter a rectangular dish. Place 4 crescent rolls rolled out flat in pan. Place sausage mixture on rolls. Spread evenly. Top with remaining crescent rolls rolled out flat. Bake for 20 minutes.
*Makes 4 servings.*

# Sausage Casserole
*Betty Givens*

1 pound bulk pork sausage, browned
1 small sweet green pepper, chopped
1 small onion, chopped
1 4-ounce can chopped pimientos with liquid
1 10¾-ounce can cream of chicken soup, undiluted
1 cup instant rice, uncooked
1 4-ounce can mushrooms

Preheat oven to 350°. Mix all ingredients well. Spoon into greased casserole dish. Bake for 35 minutes.
*Makes 4 servings.*

# Tortilla Pizza
*Ms. Fisher's 7th/8th Grade English Class*
*Smith County High School*

Soft tortillas
Tomato flavor pizza sauce
Favorite pizza toppings
   (You may want to pre-cook certain
   toppings.)
Shredded mozzarella cheese

Preheat oven to 350°. Place tortillas on a cookie sheet. Spoon pizza sauce onto each tortilla. Spread around to lightly cover the tortilla. Add your favorite toppings and sprinkle with mozzarella cheese.

Bake for about 10 minutes or until cheese is melted. Remove from oven and let cool for 2 to 3 minutes. Remove from pan and serve.
*Makes 4 to 6 servings.*

# Food: From Politics to Religion

big dinners, but now we spread them in front of the air conditioners in the fellowship halls."

Barbecue and fried fish will always reign with fried chicken as Smith County favorites. "Friday night is still, and always will be, catfish night around here," said James. "If I had to put my finger on a Carthage tradition, I'd say it's food."

Everything we do around here seems to go with food—political announcements, festivals, honors, church fellowships, and exhibits. Even plain old meetings seem to end up at the City Cafe around plate-sized hamburgers and iced tea. "I believe breaking bread together does something good for people."

For a true taste of Carthage, longtime attorney James Bass says you must attend the annual Democratic Party Barbecue. The traditional feast is held along the river just before the general election in August.

"This summer event draws all the politicals—local, state, and national, including the Gores," said James. "It was a spread that Al Sr. never missed. The Vice President comes occasionally, and Tipper came by herself once." It's just too good to miss.

Other food traditions still honored in Carthage include all-day singing and dinner on the ground at the churches. "In the old days we literally ate outdoors on the ground," Bass said. "We still have the

## Kina's Burritos
*Kina Sadler*

2 pounds ground beef
1 package tortillas
1 cup tomatoes, chopped
1 cup cheese, shredded
2 cups lettuce, shredded
1 8-ounce carton sour cream
1 onion, diced, optional

Sauté ground beef; drain. Heat tortillas for 5 to 7 minutes. Spread with tomatoes, cheese, and lettuce. Top with sour cream and onion, if desired. Roll up and eat.
*Makes 8 servings.*

## Taco Rice Casserole
*Anne B. Ratledge*

1 pound ground beef
½ cup onion, chopped
¼ cup green pepper, chopped
1 package taco seasoning mix
1½ cups water
1 8-ounce can tomato sauce
3 cups cooked rice
1 cup Velveeta cheese
1½ cups crushed taco chips

Preheat oven to 350°. Brown ground beef, onion, and peppers. Add taco seasoning and water. Cook at least 5 minutes. Add tomato sauce and cooked rice. Place in a 2-quart serving dish. Bake for 15 to 20 minutes or until heated through. Add crushed taco chips on top of casserole.
*Makes 4 servings.*

## Low-Fat! Fish "Fry"

1 egg white
⅓ cup dried bread crumbs
2 tablespoons grated Parmesan cheese
¾ teaspoon dried basil leaves
¼ teaspoon pepper
½ teaspoon salt
4 6-ounce cod filets
½ cup nonfat mayonnaise dressing
¼ cup dill pickles, finely chopped
1 tablespoon chopped parsley
2 teaspoons lemon juice
1½ teaspoons hot pepper sauce
Basil sprigs
Lemon wedges

Preheat oven to 450°. In pie plate, with fork, beat egg white slightly. On wax paper, mix bread crumbs, Parmesan cheese, dried basil, pepper, and salt. Dip cod filets in egg white, then bread crumb mixture to coat.

Place cod filets on ungreased cookie sheet. Bake for 10 to 12 minutes, without turning fish, until fish flakes easily when tested with a fork. Garnish with basil and lemon wedges.
*Makes 4 servings.*

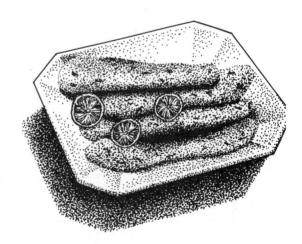

*The New Salem Baptist Church in Elmwood is where the Gores attend church when they are in Carthage on a Sunday. It was here that the funeral service for Al Sr. was held.*

# Tennessee Fried Catfish

Salt and pepper to taste
6 pan-dressed catfish
2 eggs
2 tablespoons milk
2 cups corn meal
¼ cup all-purpose flour
Vegetable oil

Salt and pepper fish. In mixing bowl, beat eggs and pour in milk. In a separate bowl, combine corn meal and flour. Dip fish in egg mixture, then coat with corn meal and flour mixture. Deep-fry fish in hot oil about 10 minutes or until brown. Take up fish and drain on paper towels. Serve hot with hushpuppies and cole slaw. This is good eatin'!
*Makes 6 servings.*

# White House Lemon Herbed Salmon

2½ cups fresh bread crumbs
4 garlic cloves, minced
½ cup fresh parsley, chopped
6 tablespoons grated Parmesan cheese
¼ cup fresh thyme, chopped or
1 tablespoon dried thyme
2 teaspoons grated lemon rind
½ teaspoon salt
6 tablespoons butter or margarine, melted and divided
1 3- to 4-pound salmon filet

Preheat oven to 350°. In a bowl, combine bread crumbs, garlic, parsley, cheese, thyme, lemon rind, and salt; mix well. Add 4 tablespoons butter and toss lightly to coat; set aside. Pat salmon dry. Place skin-side down in a greased baking dish. Brush with remaining butter; cover with crumb mixture. Bake for 20 to 25 minutes or until salmon flakes easily with a fork.
*Makes 8 servings.*

# Catfish Stir Fry

1½ pounds catfish, cut in filet strips
2 tablespoons lemon juice
4 tablespoons soy sauce
3 tablespoons vegetable oil, divided
1 cup broccoli, sliced
1 cup carrots, sliced
1 cup cauliflower, sliced
1 cup zucchini, sliced
½ cup celery, sliced
1 cup mushrooms, sliced
¼ cup green onions, sliced
½ cup water chestnuts, sliced
3 tablespoons cornstarch
1 cup water
3 cups hot, cooked rice

Marinate fish with lemon juice and soy sauce. Heat 2 tablespoons vegetable oil in large skillet; add vegetables and stir-fry for 3 minutes. Remove vegetables. Drain and reserve marinade. Stir-fry fish strips in skillet with 1 tablespoon oil, about 3 minutes. Mix cornstarch, water, and marinade; pour over vegetables. Place vegetables in skillet with fish and cook about 2 or 3 minutes or until sauce has thickened. Serve hot over rice.
*Makes 4 servings.*

*After voting in 1996, Al and Tipper pose for a picture with students at Forks River School, which is down the road from their house.*

# Flounder Casserole

1 cup celery, chopped
½ stick butter or margarine, melted
2 cups cooked, flaked flounder or other fish
1 10¾-ounce can condensed cream of
    mushroom soup
1 cup cracker crumbs
3 hard-boiled eggs, chopped
¾ cup shredded Cheddar cheese, divided
Paprika

Preheat oven to 375°. In a 10-inch skillet, cook celery in butter until tender; remove from heat. Add fish, soup, cracker crumbs, eggs, and ¼ cup cheese; mix well. Place fish mixture in a well-greased 1½-quart casserole. Sprinkle with remaining cheese and paprika. Bake for 20 to 25 minutes or until thoroughly heated and cheese is melted.

*Makes 6 servings.*

# VEGETABLES & SIDE DISHES

Nothing is so refreshing and delicious as the feast of vegetables that grace the tables of Middle-Tennessee cooks. Maybe it's because gardening is part of our lifestyle or because learning to cook the wide variety of available vegetables in a myriad of ways is part of becoming a cook in the South.

Why are Southern vegetable dishes so tempting? Is it because we cook them until they are so soft and savory that the thought of them makes us salivate? Is it the little secrets that Southern cooks use, like putting a spoonful of bacon grease in the pot to add flavor? Is it frying them instead of boiling them? Whatever it is, Southern vegetable dishes are tasty.

Vegetables are easy to fix. But don't tell anyone, because these recipes will make you look like a gourmet chef at the next church social.

## Apple Dumplings
*Rachel Elrod*

⅓ cup firmly packed brown sugar
¼ cup butter, melted
1 teaspoon cinnamon
1 recipe dough for double-crust pie
6 small baking apples, peeled and cored
¼ cup apple jelly
1½ cups sugar
1½ cups water

Preheat oven to 350°. Combine the brown sugar, butter, and cinnamon in a bowl; set aside. Divide the pastry into 6 equal portions. Roll out each portion on a floured surface to form a 6-inch square. Place an apple in the center of each square. Fill the center of each apple with 2 teaspoons jelly. Spread the brown sugar mixture on top of the apples in the pastry and place into a 9x13-inch baking pan. Bake for about 30 minutes or until the apples are tender. Combine the sugar and water in a saucepan. Bring to a boil. Pour over the dumplings. Bake for 10 minutes, basting the dumplings occasionally with syrup.
*Makes 6 servings.*

## Maple Baked Apples

2 medium cooking apples
2 tablespoons raisins
2 tablespoons chopped pecans
½ cup maple syrup
2 tablespoons butter or margarine, divided
¼ cup water

Preheat oven to 350°. Core apples, peel top third of each. Place apples in a shallow baking dish. Combine raisins, pecans, and cinnamon. Fill cavities of apples with mixture.

Pour maple syrup over apples; top each with 1 tablespoon butter. Pour water into bottom of dish. Cover and bake for 45 to 50 minutes or until apples are tender.
*Makes 2 servings.*

## Fried Apples

3 tablespoons butter or margarine
3 medium unpeeled tart apples, cored quartered, and sliced
⅓ cup sugar
2 to 4 tablespoons sugar

Melt butter in skillet over medium heat. Add apples to skillet; cover and cook 5 minutes or until they are juicy. Turn apples; sprinkle with the ⅓ cup sugar. Reduce heat to medium low. Cover apples; cook 4 or 5 minutes. Uncover and cook until sugar is absorbed and apples are lightly browned on bottom, 3 to 4 minutes. Remove from heat; sprinkle apples with 2 to 4 tablespoons sugar. Serve hot.
*Makes 4 servings.*

## Asparagus and Pea Casserole
*Wilma Fisher*

1 16-ounce can green peas, drained
2 hard-boiled eggs, sliced
1 15-ounce can asparagus spears
1 cup grated American cheese
1 10¾-ounce can cream of mushroom soup
¼ cup onion, finely chopped
¼ cup almonds, slivered
1 cup cracker crumbs
Butter

Preheat oven to 350°. Butter a medium baking dish. Pour green peas into dish. Add layer of sliced eggs. Add asparagus, then layer of eggs. Add cheese to mushroom soup and heat until cheese is melted. Add onion to mixture and pour over layers. Sprinkle almonds and cracker crumbs on top. Dot with butter. Bake for about 30 minutes or until bubbly.

*Makes 4 servings.*

# Asparagus Casserole
*Mary Blackwell*

2  15-ounce cans asparagus spears
1  9-ounce can water chestnuts, sliced
1  8-ounce can mushrooms, sliced
1  3-ounce can chopped pimientos
4  hard-boiled eggs, chopped
1  10¾-ounce can mushroom soup

Preheat oven to 350°. Drain asparagus, arrange in greased casserole dish. Drain water chestnuts, mushrooms, and pimientos. Add chopped egg to soup. Stir in drained ingredients and pour over asparagus. Bake for 25 minutes. Also good topped with French-fried onions or shredded Cheddar cheese.

*Makes 6 to 8 servings.*

*Civic-minded postal workers in Carthage stock shelves at the local Food Bank that assists people in the area who are in need.*

# Barbecue Baked Beans
*Vickey Fields*

1 pound ground beef
3 slices bacon
1 28-ounce can pork and beans
4 tablespoons catsup
2 tablespoons brown sugar
1 small onion, diced
½ cup barbeque sauce

Brown ground beef and drain. Cook bacon slices. Combine all ingredients and place in baking dish. Bake 45 minutes to 1 hour.
*Makes 8 servings.*

# Broccoli Stuffing Casserole
*O'geal Carter*

4 10-ounce packages frozen broccoli
1 10¾-ounce can cream of mushroom soup
1 10¾-ounce can cream of chicken soup
2 cups herbed seasoned stuffing mix
½ stick margarine

Preheat oven to 325°. Cook broccoli according to package directions. Drain and place half the mixture into a 9x13-inch baking dish. Top with half the mushroom soup and half the cream of chicken soup. Repeat layers. Top with stuffing mix and dot with margarine. Bake for 20 minutes or until bubbly.
*Makes 2 to 4 servings.*

# Broccoli Casserole
*Lois Martin*

1 10-ounce package frozen chopped broccoli
½ stick margarine
1 8-ounce jar of Cheez Whiz
1 10¾-ounce can cream of mushroom soup
1½ cups Minute Rice

Preheat oven to 350° (if using metal pan), 325° (if using glass dish). Cook frozen chopped broccoli according to package directions. Drain off all water. Add margarine, Cheez Whiz, mushroom soup, and Minute Rice. Mix well. Pour into casserole dish sprayed with nonstick cooking spray. Bake for 30 to 45 minutes.
*Makes 2 to 4 servings.*

# Potato-Broccoli Casserole
*Mary Blackwell*

4 medium potatoes, diced
1 medium onion, chopped
1 10-ounce package broccoli, cooked and drained
Salt and pepper to taste
½ stick margarine
1 10¾-ounce can cream of mushroom soup
½ to 1 cup grated cheese

Boil potatoes until done. Drain; add onion and place in a casserole dish. Add cooked broccoli, salt, and pepper. Top with margarine and soup, cover with cheese. Bake for about 20 minutes or until bubbly and cheese is melted.
*Makes 4 servings.*

## Aunt Dona Rankin's Cabbage Casserole

1 medium cabbage
1 medium onion, diced
1 10¾-ounce can cream of celery soup
Shredded Cheddar cheese
Bread crumbs
1 pound ground beef

Cook and drain ground beef. In large casserole dish, layer cabbage, onion, beef, soup, and cheese alternately. Sprinkle bread crumbs on top. Cook in oven at 350° for 1 hour.
*Makes 6 to 8 servings.*

## Cabbage Rolls

1 pound ground beef
¼ cup onions, chopped
1 cup cooked rice
1 teaspoon salt
1 egg, beaten
8 large cabbage leaves
1 16-ounce can tomato sauce
1 tablespoon brown sugar
½ teaspoon basil leaves
½ teaspoon oregano leaves

Combine first 5 ingredients well. Divide into 8 equal parts and wrap cabbage leaf around each portion; secure with a toothpick. Place in a glass dish. Combine remaining ingredients and pour over rolls. Cover with wax paper. Microwave on High for 8 minutes. Baste rolls with sauce; rotate dish ½ turn and recover. Microwave 6½ to 8½ minutes, or until meat is set.
   *Tip:* To remove cabbage leaves, microwave the whole cabbage head 1½ to 3½ minutes, until 8 outer leaves can be easily removed. Refrigerate remaining cabbage for future use.
*Makes 4 servings.*

## Glorified Sauerkraut
*Louise Blackburn*

2 to 3 onions, chopped
1 green pepper, chopped
1 4-ounce can mushrooms, drained
Butter
1 16-ounce can sauerkraut, drained
1 16-ounce can tomatoes, chopped
1½ teaspoons sugar

Preheat oven to 350°. Sauté onions, green peppers, and mushrooms in butter for a few minutes until they are lightly cooked. Drain excess liquid. In a casserole dish, combine all ingredients. Bake, covered, for 1 hour. Remove cover and continue baking 30 minutes longer.
*Makes 6 to 8 servings.*

## Corn Casserole
*BeLinda Watts*

2 12-ounce cans white corn
1 16-ounce can French-style green beans
½ cup onions, chopped
½ cup celery, chopped
½ cup green peppers, chopped
¾ cup grated sharp cheese
1 10¾-ounce can cream of celery soup
1 8-ounce carton sour cream
1 stick margarine
1 stack butter flavored crackers, crushed

Preheat oven to 350°. Thoroughly mix all ingredients, except margarine and crackers. Place in 9x13-inch casserole dish. Melt margarine and mix with crushed crackers; spread evenly over the vegetable mixture. Bake for about 45 minutes.
*Makes about 12 to 15 servings.*

# Miss Mattie's Chicken

To really learn about Carthage lifestyles and foods, one of the best people to turn to is Mattie Payne, who started working for the Al Gore family when she was six years old. Now eighty-seven, Miss Mattie is one of those special people who grows kinder for every year of service she offers so unselfishly.

For years Mattie was a teacher in Carthage and Forks River Elementary School. Then she worked for more than thirty years for the Gore family cooking and keeping the house while the family was away. Now she works ceaselessly for senior citizens, the sick . . . and the Democrats.

When the Gore family built their new home, they included a room for Miss Mattie. Pauline Gore wrote, "Mattie Payne has been my housekeeper and kitchen supervisor for about thirty years. She has also been a confidante of each member of our family, beloved by all. Most of all, the grandchildren love her. They know they can depend on Mattie to have what they like best to eat, as well as to listen to all their problems. During our years in Washington, Mattie, who has a Master's degree in education, taught in the Smith County schools and kept watch on our house while we were away.

"For about thirty years, Mattie and I have had annual cattle sale parties for a hundred to three hundred people, lunch for two hundred to five hundred, and snacks after the sale for fifty to a hundred. We have worked out favorite recipes for large crowds.

"Not many years ago, my grandchildren were coming to Tennessee for a week, so I asked what they would like for dinner the first night home. In a chorus they said, 'Mattie's chicken!' Then Karenna, the oldest, added, 'The *first* night and the *second* night and the *last* night.'

"I think their very favorite meal is Mattie's fried chicken, cheese potatoes, green beans, fresh fried corn in season, squash, a salad, homemade cornbread, loaf bread, chocolate ice cream and yellow cake."

Miss Mattie is very modest about Miss Pauline's feeling for her. She prefers to talk about the Gore children and their appetites. Special events such as birthdays and Christmas are fond memories that revolve around food. Traditional dressing and ham are family favorites. Cake was the favorite dessert, Miss Mattie recalls. "Al Jr.'s favorite is coconut cake," she says. "And Mr. Gore Sr. would eat anything," she laughed. "If I put it on the table, he'd eat it."

## Corn Casserole
*Dorothy Hitchcock*

2 16-ounce cans whole kernel corn
1 10¾-ounce can cream of celery soup
½ cup onion, finely chopped
½ cup green pepper, finely chopped
1 3-ounce jar pimientos, diced
½ cup sour cream
Ritz crackers

Preheat oven to 350°. Drain corn, add next 5 ingredients. Stir well. Pour into casserole dish. Crumble a generous amount of crackers on top. Bake for 40 minutes or until bubbly.
*Makes 6 to 8 servings.*

## Easy Sweet Corn Soufflé
*Peggy Chapman*

1 16-ounce can cream corn
3 eggs, beaten
1 cup milk
1 tablespoon cornstarch
2 tablespoons sugar
1 stick butter or margarine, melted
½ cup sugar
½ cup water
1 tablespoon all-purpose flour

Preheat oven to 350°. Mix first 5 ingredients together. Bake for 1 hour or until a knife inserted in the center comes out clean. Mix butter, sugar, water, and flour. Heat in pan stirring until well blended. Pour on top of soufflé just before serving.
*Makes 4 servings.*

## Sesame Green Beans
*Margaret Stone*

¾ pound fresh green beans
½ cup water
1 tablespoon butter or margarine
1 tablespoon soy sauce
2 teaspoons toasted sesame seeds

In saucepan, bring beans and water to boil. Reduce heat to medium. Cover and cook for 10 to 15 minutes, or until the beans are tender. Drain. Add butter, soy sauce, and sesame seeds. Toss to coat.
*Makes 3 to 4 servings.*

## Green Bean Casserole
*Lucy Hackett Oldham*

1 medium onion, diced
2 tablespoons margarine
1 10¾-ounce can mushroom soup
2 16-ounce cans French-style green beans, drained
Approximately 1 cup cheese, grated (Cheddar or Velveeta)
Chinese noodles

Preheat oven to 325°. Cook onion in margarine until clear. Stir in soup and beans. Heat thoroughly. In a 1-quart casserole dish, place a layer of this mixture and a layer of grated cheese; repeat. Top with Chinese noodles, or if preferred, bake casserole for 10 to 12 minutes and then add noodles so they will not become too crunchy during baking. Continue to bake for another 10 to 12 minutes or until bubbly. If Cheddar cheese is used, baking time will take a little longer.
*Makes 8 servings.*

## Sandy's Green Bean Casserole
*Sandy Stafford*

1 10¾-ounce can cream of mushroom soup
½ cup milk
1 teaspoon soy sauce
2 dashes of pepper
4 cups cooked French-style green beans
1⅓ cups French-fried onions

Preheat oven to 350°. Mix soup, milk, soy sauce, pepper, beans, and ⅔ cup onions in 1½-quart casserole dish. Bake for 25 minutes. Stir and sprinkle on remaining onions. Bake 5 minutes longer.
*Makes 4 to 6 servings.*

## Onion Shortbread Casserole
*O'geal Carter*

1 8-ounce package cornbread mix
⅓ cup milk
1 egg, beaten
2 large onions, sliced
Vegetable oil
¼ cup mayonnaise
1 16-ounce can cream-style corn
1 cup sour cream
1 cup shredded Cheddar cheese, divided
1 teaspoon salt
½ cup mayonnaise
Cayenne pepper or Tabasco sauce to taste

Preheat oven to 350°. Combine cornbread mix, mayonnaise, milk, and egg in bowl; mix well and spread evenly into a 9x13-inch baking pan. Sauté onion in small amount of oil or nonstick skillet until tender. Arrange over cornbread mixture. Combine corn, sour cream, ¾ cup Cheddar cheese, salt, mayonnaise, and cayenne pepper in bowl. Mix well. Spoon over onion layer. Top with remaining cheese. Bake for 30 minutes.
*Makes 12 servings.*

## Stuffed Green Peppers
*Glenda Jones*

2 large green peppers, cut in half and seeded
1 pound hamburger
1 cup cooked rice
1 8-ounce can tomato sauce
Salt and pepper to taste
Parmesan cheese

Preheat oven to 350°. Cook green peppers in boiling water until tender. During this time, brown meat and drain. Add rice, tomato sauce, salt, and pepper. Drain peppers and add meat mixture. Place in dish and sprinkle with Parmesan cheese. Bake until heated through and cheese is bubbly.
*Makes 2 servings.*

## Pinto Beans
*Sharon Raines*

2 cups dry pinto beans
Water
2 tablespoons salt
¼ cup bacon drippings

Wash pinto beans and put in crock pot. Add enough warm water to fill crock pot over beans (about 2½ quarts). Add salt and drippings.

Cook on High for 6 to 8 hours. Stir and serve with cornbread and onion slices.
*Makes 6 to 8 servings.*

*The Al Gore Sr. family, baggage in hand, left their temporary home at the Skyline apartments in Washington, D.C. in 1952 to return to their home in Carthage for an extended stay. From left, Nancy 14, Pauline Gore, Albert 4, and Al Gore Sr.*

# Pinto Beans and Ham Hock

1 smoked ham hock
Water
1 teaspoon salt
2 cups dried pinto beans
1 cup onion, coarsely chopped
¼ teaspoon pepper

Place ham hock and salt in large Dutch oven or saucepot. Add enough water to cover. Cook ham, covered, over moderately high heat until water comes to a boil. Reduce heat to medium low and cook for 30 minutes. Add beans, onion, and pepper to ham and cook, covered, for approximately 3½ hours or until beans are tender. Remove meat from the ham bone and serve a little of the meat with each serving.
*Makes 6 servings.*

# Hazel's Cheesy Goulash
*Beverly Gillispie*

8 medium potatoes
Water
1 stick butter
1 8-ounce box macaroni noodles
2 10¾-ounce cans cream of chicken soup
1 pound Velveeta cheese, cubed

Peel and cube potatoes, cover with water, and bring to a boil. After potatoes have boiled for 10 minutes, add butter and noodles. Cook until potatoes and noodles are done and water is just above mixture. Add mixture of soup and cheese. Turn on low heat and stir until cheese has melted and soup is well blended.
*Makes 8 servings.*

# Hashbrown Casserole
*Debra Hensley*

1 10¾-ounce can cream of chicken soup
8 ounces grated Colby cheese
1 small onion, chopped
5 tablespoons margarine, melted
¾ teaspoon black pepper
1 teaspoon salt
2 pounds frozen shredded potatoes

Preheat oven to 350°. In a large mixing bowl, combine soup, cheese, onions, margarine, salt, and pepper. Mix together well. Add potatoes (do not pre-thaw). Bake, uncovered, for 30 minutes.
*Makes 8 to 10 servings.*

# Sour Cream and Onion Potatoes
*Molly M. Bowman*

1 medium onion, chopped
1 stick margarine
4 medium potatoes, diced
1 cup milk
1 cup sour cream

Brown onion in margarine. Add potatoes. Fry, covered, until slightly tender and golden. Stir frequently. Add milk. Turn heat down to a slow simmer. Cook, covered, for 30 minutes. Add sour cream. Recipe may be doubled.
*Makes 3 to 4 servings.*

## Potatoes for the Grill

*Beverly Gillispie*

8 potatoes
1 large green pepper
1 large onion, sliced
1 stick butter
Salt
Pepper

Peel potatoes, slice green peppers and onion. Drain mushrooms and slice butter over the top of all your vegetables. Salt and pepper to taste. Wrap tightly in foil. Cook on grill 2 hours. This can also be done in an oven.
*Makes 8 servings.*

## Potato Fritters

Potatoes
4 tablespoons butter, softened to room
    temperature
4 egg yolks, lightly beaten
Dash of nutmeg
Salt and pepper to taste
1¼ cups all-purpose flour
1 cup tepid water
2 tablespoons olive oil
1 tablespoon brandy
1 egg yolk
Pinch of salt
½ teaspoon baking powder
1 egg white, stiffly beaten

Peel and cook enough potatoes to make 2½ cups after they have been put through a ricer. Combine the potatoes with softened butter, 4 egg yolks, nutmeg, salt, and pepper to taste.

Beat the mixture until it is well blended and smooth. Chill.

Mix together flour, tepid water, olive oil, brandy, 1 egg yolk, and a pinch of salt. Stir until the batter is smooth and when ready to use, add baking powder and stiffly beaten egg white.

Form the chilled potato mixture into small balls. Dip them into the batter and fry a few at a time in hot deep fat (375°) until they are golden brown. Drain the balls on paper towels, serve hot.
*Makes 6 to 8 servings.*

*At the Smith County Fall Heritage Festival each October, craftsmen like this man making a broom show how life used to be in Carthage.*

# Down-Home Beans and Potatoes

1½ pounds fresh green beans
8 slices bacon, quartered
1 small onion, chopped
5 cups water
1 teaspoon salt
½ teaspoon pepper
1½ cups cubed red potatoes

Wash beans; trim ends, and remove strings. Cut into 1½-inch pieces; set aside. Fry bacon until crisp in a Dutch oven. Remove bacon and set aside; reserve ¼ cup bacon drippings in Dutch oven. Sauté onion in drippings until tender.

Add water to onion; bring to a boil. Add bacon, beans, salt, and pepper, and return to a boil. Cover and simmer 15 minutes. Add potatoes, and cook 10 minutes or until potatoes are tender. Drain.
*Makes 6 servings.*

# Candied Sweet Potatoes
*Christy Scudder*

8 to 10 sweet potatoes
1 cup white corn syrup
1 cup maple syrup
1 teaspoon vanilla extract
1 stick margarine
Water to moisten

Boil potatoes for 15 to 20 minutes and peel. Place in a 9x13-inch baking dish. Preheat oven to 350°. Combine next 5 ingredients in small saucepan. Bring to a boil, stirring constantly. Pour syrup over potatoes. Bake for at least 1 hour. These store well in the refrigerator and are great warmed over.
*Makes 8 to 10 servings.*

# Tennessee Sweet Potato Casserole
*Molly M. Bowman*

6 to 7 medium to large sweet potatoes, sliced, or 2 large cans sweet potatoes
½ cup milk
½ cup raisins
½ cup coconut
1 cup sugar
½ stick margarine
1 tablespoon vanilla extract
Rice Krispies
Marshmallows

Cook potatoes till done. Drain, peel, and mash. Add next 6 ingredients. Mix well. Pour into casserole dish. Layer on Rice Krispies, then marshmallows. Bake until golden brown.
*Makes 6 to 8 servings.*

# Yum Yum Sweet Potato Casserole
*Roberta Williams*

3 cups cooked sweet potatoes, mashed
1 stick butter, melted
2 eggs, beaten
1 tablespoon vanilla extract
1 cup firmly packed brown sugar
⅓ cup all-purpose flour
1 cup chopped pecans
⅓ cup butter, softened to room temperature

Preheat oven to 350°. In large bowl, mix together sweet potatoes, butter, eggs, and vanilla extract. Pour into casserole dish. Combine remaining ingredients and sprinkle over casserole. Bake for 20 minutes.
*Makes 6 to 8 servings.*

# Cordell Hull Lake

If you take a leisurely drive to the north of Carthage, you'll find beautiful 12,000-acre Cordell Hull Lake. It's named for one of America's outstanding statesmen, Cordell Hull, who was often called the Father of the United Nations. A tourist brochure says the lake's excellent recreational facilities are operated primarily for the purposes of navigation, hydropower and recreation. The people in Carthage think of it as a place for fun and good times.

There are two beautiful marinas and the Corps of Engineers have built six recreation areas. You can kick your boat into high and do a little skiing, or slide it into slow and catch a few fish to fry. You might even decide to go walking, hunting, or camping in the forest around the lake. There's 20,000 acres of scenic public land that surround it.

And don't forget to bring your picnic lunch! There are lots of great spots to spread out a blanket, have a picnic, read a book, or take a nap in the shade. Cordell Hull Lake is one of Carthage's most relaxing spots.

# Apple and Raisin Stuffing

1 cup onions, chopped (and their juice)
7 cups soft bread crumbs
3 cups peeled, cored, and cubed apples
1 cup parboiled seedless raisins, drained and
    dried
½ cup parsley leaves, finely chopped
1½ teaspoons salt
½ teaspoon powdered mace
½ teaspoon sage
½ teaspoon nutmeg
½ teaspoon cloves
1 clove garlic, finely chopped
1½ sticks butter, melted

Combine all ingredients. Blend thoroughly.
Use to stuff a turkey.
*Makes about 10–12 servings.*

# Cranberry Stuffing for Roast Pork

1½ cups raw cranberries
4 cups cooked wild rice
⅓ cup butter, melted
3 to 4 tablespoons sugar (or to taste)
2 tablespoons grated onion
1 teaspoon salt
½ teaspoon sweet marjoram
1 clove of garlic, mashed
Generous pinch each of black pepper, mace,
    thyme, and dill

Put cranberries through a food chopper, using
the coarsest blade. In a saucepan, combine the
cranberries with remaining ingredients. Mix
the stuffing well and cook it over medium heat
for about 10 minutes, stirring constantly.

Cool the stuffing before filling a crown
roast of pork.
*Makes about 5 cups.*

# Sausage and Sweet Potato Stuffing

½ pound sausage
1 medium onion, finely minced or grated
¾ cup celery tops, finely chopped
4 cups hot sweet potatoes, mashed
2 cups stale bread crumbs
½ cup fresh mushrooms, finely chopped
2 generous teaspoons salt
½ teaspoon black pepper
½ teaspoon nutmeg
Pinch of thyme
Pinch of cloves

Sauté sausage meat until it is lightly browned,
breaking it into small pieces as it cooks. Remove
the meat from the pan. In the drippings, sauté
the onion and celery tops. Add sweet potatoes,
bread crumbs, mushrooms, salt, black pepper,
nutmeg, thyme, and cloves. Combine the
mixture thoroughly. Add the cooked sausage
meat and heat through. Cool the stuffing before
using.

*Makes enough to stuff a chicken; recipe can be doubled
or tripled for turkey.*

# Alota Thompson's Cornbread Dressing

*Sue Thompson*

4 to 5 cups cornbread, cooked and crumbled
1 can biscuits (10), baked
1½ cups onions, chopped
2 cups celery, chopped
1 tablespoon sage
2 cups water
1 cup chicken or turkey broth

Salt and pepper to taste
2 eggs, beaten

Preheat oven to 300°. Crumble cornbread and biscuits into a large pot. Combine all remaining ingredients, except eggs, in a saucepan. Let boil for 10 minutes and pour over the bread crumbs. Add the eggs, mixing well. Place the dressing in a greased baking dish. Bake for 30 minutes.

*Makes 10 to 12 servings.*

*In 1992 Carthage celebrated the Clinton-Gore election by sending the Smith County High School band to Washington, D.C., to march in the inaugural parade.*

# Cornbread-Sausage Dressing

1 cup pecan halves
7½ slices toasted bread, torn
6 cups cornbread crumbs
6 chicken-flavored bouillon cubes
4 cups boiling water
1 small onion, quartered
2 green peppers, cored, seeded, and
    quartered
2 stalks celery, cut into 3-inch pieces
½ stick butter or margarine, melted
½ pound bulk pork sausage
1 teaspoon poultry seasoning
½ teaspoon salt
¼ teaspoon pepper
4 eggs, beaten

Position knife blade in food processor bowl. Add pecans, top with cover, and pulse 10 times or until finely chopped. Remove pecans and set aside.

Place toast pieces in processor bowl; process until coarsely crumbled. Combine with cornbread crumbs in a large bowl. Dissolve bouillon cubes in boiling water; pour over crumb mixture, and stir well.

Place onion in processor bowl, top with cover and pulse 4 to 5 times or until coarsely chopped. Add green pepper through food chute; pulse 6 times or until onion and pepper are finely chopped. Remove knife blade, leaving vegetables in processor bowl. Position shredding disc in processor bowl; top with cover. Place celery pieces in food chute; shred celery, using medium pressure.

Remove vegetables from processor, and sauté in butter until tender; add to crumb mixture, stirring well. Preheat oven to 350°.

Brown sausage in a heavy skillet; drain. Stir sausage and remaining ingredients into cornbread mixture. Spoon into a lightly greased 13x9x2-inch baking dish; bake for about 45 minutes.

*Makes 8 to 10 servings.*

*This 1991 photo from* The Tennessean *pictures (from left to right) Sherry Jo Anderson, Helen Wilburn, and Leslie Alford in Norma's Cafe talking about whether Al Gore Jr. would run for president or not.*

## Squash Dressing
*Mozella Page*

3 cups cooked squash, drained
3 cups cornbread crumbs
3 eggs, beaten
1 medium onion, chopped
1 stick margarine, melted
1 10¾-ounce can cream of chicken soup

Preheat oven to 350°. Mix all ingredients together. Place in baking dish for 30 minutes.
*Makes 6 to 8 servings.*

## Squash Casserole
*O'geal Carter*

3 cups cornbread stuffing mix
½ stick margarine, melted
1 10¾-ounce can cream of chicken soup
2 small yellow squash, shredded
¼ cup carrots, shredded
2 small zucchini, shredded
½ cup Cheddar cheese, shredded
½ cup sour cream

Preheat oven to 350°. Mix stuffing and margarine, reserving ½ stuffing mixture. Place remaining stuffing mixture in a 2-quart baking dish. Mix soup, yellow squash, carrots, zucchini, cheese, and sour cream. Spread over stuffing mixture. Sprinkle reserved stuffing mixture over soup mixture. Bake for 35 minutes or until heated through.
*Makes 4 to 6 servings.*

## Batter-Dipped Fried Tomatoes
*Millie Gwaltney*

4 half-ripe medium tomatoes
½ cup all-purpose flour
2½ teaspoons salt
2½ teaspoons sugar
Pepper to taste
¾ cup evaporated milk
Vegetable oil

Wash tomatoes, but do not peel. Cut into ¾-inch slices. Place on paper towels to drain. Combine flour, salt, sugar, and pepper. Blend in milk to make a thick batter. Dip floured tomatoes in batter. Fry in ½-inch deep hot oil until golden brown on both sides.
*Makes 6 servings.*

## Fried Green Tomatoes

1 medium tomato for each person
Corn meal
Bacon drippings
Salt and pepper to taste

Slice tomatoes ¼-inch thick and roll in corn meal. Fry in bacon drippings and sprinkle with salt and pepper. Serve hot.
   *Note:* Served piping hot is best. Red or green tomatoes can be used.

# The Best Food in Town

"The best place in town to eat," said an antique dealer, pointing out his window, "is the jailhouse just across the square." A postman confirmed the opinion. "The best food in Carthage is at the jailhouse, just over there on the southwest side of the square."

By now you've probably decided that "the jailhouse" is the name of an eatery. But across the square is a big sign that reads "Smith County Sheriff and Jail."

Determined to see this through, you step into the lobby of the two-story building and approach a deputy sheriff.

"I know you'll think this is a strange question, but I've been told the best place to eat in Carthage is the jailhouse. But this seems to be a *real* jailhouse. Can you tell me where the café might be?"

The deputy laughs, "You've come to the right place. Follow me." The deputy walks down the hall past an obvious interrogation area, past a booking room and through a lobby. Suddenly the aroma of breakfast floods your nostrils, and the deputy indicates you are to enter the door he is near.

You have to remind yourself firmly that you are in the county jail because the first thing you see is a long table flanked by high-backed chairs. The table is set elegantly with placemats, china, silverware, and candles!

On the spanking-clean counter is a tray of breakfast leftovers with fat sausage patties, crisp bacon, fluffy biscuits and scrambled eggs.

You smile at the lady near the big restaurant-style stove and say, "I thought this really was a jail!"

"It sure is," the lady laughs. "I just like to make eating my food a good experience. I always set the table as if company is coming."

And company does come. Mattie Smith has cooked for more than seven years for the inmates in the Smith County Jail. The women are served in their quarters on the first floor and the men are served in the basement. The attractive setting in the kitchen on the first floor is for staff and visitors. She explains that guests range from visiting dignitaries to the jurors serving on a high-profile trial at the Smith County Courthouse.

Mattie Smith likes cooking for inmates. She says their favorite foods are fried chicken, meat loaf and roast beef.

"I just cook as I did at home," she says. "I had eight children, and if you can cook for eight, you can cook for thirty."

Mattie Smith brushes aside compliments on her super-clean, airy kitchen complete with ruffled curtains at the barred windows. She says the jail trustees do the cleaning and dishwashing. She does the shopping, often using donated vegetables and garden produce.

"I have to make the budget stretch, just as I did at home. But I have to serve well-

balanced and nutritious meals, because we are inspected by the State."

Mattie doesn't use recipes. "I use what's in my head," she says. "It comes really natural to me."

She's known some of the prisoners all her life. "I get lots of compliments from them, but I give no seconds. I fix their plates, and that's that."

Rumors have it that some prisoners get into trouble when they're released from jail just so they can come back and eat her food. Mattie just grins when you ask her if it's true.

Among the folks she's fed in the big jail kitchen are the Al Gores, both senior and junior. Al Gore Sr. was a frequent visitor, she says, and his favorite food was fried chicken.

"I'm still here and I really like it," she says when asked if she gives any thought to retirement (she's sixty-two). "I haven't got time to die if I'm busy cooking," she laughs.

Mattie Smith's determination to keep on cooking and the well-fed inmates in the Smith County Jail will help them maintain their reputation as "the best-fed prisoners in the country!"

## Saucy Turnips

6 cups peeled, sliced turnips
1¼ cups water
3 small green onions, sliced
1 tablespoon butter or margarine
1 teaspoon garlic powder
1 teaspoon seasoning salt
1 tablespoon cornstarch
¼ cup water
1 cup Cheddar cheese, shredded

Place turnips in a large saucepan; add 1¼ cups water and bring to a boil. Cover and cook for 12 minutes. Add green onions, butter, garlic powder, and salt; cook an additional 5 minutes. Dissolve cornstarch in ¼ cup water; add to turnips, stirring until combined. Add cheese; cook until cheese melts.
*Makes 6 servings.*

## Sauerkraut Relish

1 16-ounce jar sauerkraut, drained and chopped
1 small cucumber, unpeeled, finely shredded
1 small carrot, scraped and finely shredded
¼ cup sugar
¼ cup green onions, with tops, diced
2 tablespoons celery, diced
2 tablespoons green pepper, diced
2 tablespoons vinegar
2 tablespoons vegetable oil
1 tablespoon pimiento, chopped
½ teaspoon caraway seeds
⅛ teaspoon paprika
⅛ teaspoon white pepper

Combine all ingredients in a large bowl; mix well. Cover and chill. Serve with fish or cold cuts.
*Makes 3½ cups.*

## Freezer Pickles
*Virgie Mae Bass*

1 sweet pepper, chopped
3 onions, sliced
1 tablespoon mustard seed
1 tablespoon celery seed
1 tablespoon salt
1 cup white vinegar
7 large cucumbers, sliced thin

Combine first 7 ingredients in large bowl and pour over cucumbers. Put in freezer.
*Makes about 4 cups.*

## Lemon-Mint Vinegar

1 lemon
¼ cup fresh mint, chopped
2 cups white wine vinegar, 5% acidity
Sprigs of fresh mint, optional
Lemon rind strips, optional

Cut a continuous spiral of rind from lemon and place in a large wide-mouthed jar. Reserve remainder of lemon for other uses. Add ¼ cup mint to jar.

Place vinegar in a medium saucepan and bring to a boil. Pour vinegar over mint and lemon rind; cover with lid. Let stand at room temperature for 2 weeks.

Strain vinegar into decorative jars, discarding lemon and herb residue; add additional sprigs of fresh mint and lemon rind, if desired. Seal jars with a cork or other airtight lid.
*Makes 2 cups.*

# SWEET TREATS

Just about the time you think you can't hold another bite, here comes your hostess with some tempting sweet treat that you can't pass up. Strawberry shortcake with fresh strawberries and homemade whipped cream. A plate of Loren Blair's Believe-It-or-Not Cookies. Or Tipper Gore's Tennessee Treats.

Americans' desire for a sweet at the end of a meal has not been neglected by Carthage cooks. Our this-side-of-heaven candies, cookies, and other tantalizing sweet treats will have your mouth watering. And this doesn't even include pies and cakes—we have two more whole sections for them!

The SnoBiz Shave Ice stand in Carthage attracts those who live here and passersby alike who are looking for a cool treat on a hot day. When the urge hits you, come on by and enjoy your favorite flavor.

# Josh's Double Almond Butter Cookies

*Josh Brown*

4 sticks butter, softened to room temperature
2½ cups confectioner's sugar, sifted and divided
4 cups all-purpose flour
2¼ teaspoons vanilla extract, divided
⅔ cup Blue Diamond blanched almond paste
¼ cup firmly packed light brown sugar
½ cup Blue Diamond chopped natural almonds, toasted

Beat butter with 1 cup sugar. Gradually beat in flour. Beat in 2 teaspoons vanilla. Cover and chill dough for 30 minutes. Preheat oven to 350°. Combine almond paste, brown sugar, almonds, and remaining vanilla. Shape dough around ½ teaspoon almond paste mixture, completely enclosing almond paste center and forming 1-inch balls. Place on ungreased pan. Bake for 15 minutes. Cool. Roll cookies in remaining sugar or sift sugar over cookies.
*Makes 8 dozen cookies*

# Chocolate Oatmeal Cookies

*Kristy Givens*

2 cups sugar
3 tablespoons cocoa
Pinch of salt
½ stick margarine, melted
½ cup milk
½ cup peanut butter
2 cups quick-cooking oats
1 teaspoon vanilla extract

Mix sugar, cocoa, and salt; add margarine and milk. Cook on top of stove and boil for 1 minute. Take pan off heat and add the peanut butter. Stir constantly. Add oats and vanilla; mix well. Drop by the spoonful onto wax paper.
*Makes about 3 dozen.*

# Chocolate Chip Oatmeal Raisin Walnut Cookies

1 cup solid shortening
¾ cup firmly packed brown sugar
¾ cup sugar
2 eggs
1 teaspoon vanilla extract
1 teaspoon baking soda
½ cup wheat germ
1 cup rolled oats
12 ounces chocolate chips
½ cup raisins
½ cup walnuts

Preheat oven to 375°. Cream shortening, sugars, eggs, and vanilla together until light and fluffy. Sift together dry ingredients and stir into creamed mixture. Stir in wheat germ, oats, chocolate chips, raisins, and walnuts. Drop by the spoonful 2 inches apart onto greased cookie sheet. Bake for 7 to 8 minutes.
*Makes about 3 dozen.*

# Chocolate Chip Cookies
*Gloria Stewart*

½ stick butter
1 egg
1 tablespoon vanilla extract
1 cup sugar
½ cup firmly packed brown sugar
1½ cups self-rising flour
8 ounces milk chocolate chips
1 cup chopped pecans

Blend butter, egg, vanilla and sugars together in a large mixing bowl. Add flour and blend until batter becomes doughy. Fold chocolate chips and chopped pecans into dough. Preheat oven to 350°. Roll dough out on wax paper to form a 2-inch log. Refrigerate until firm or overnight. Cut into ½-inch thick slices. Cut each slice into 4 pieces. Place on ungreased cookie sheet. Bake cookies for 8 to 10 minutes or until golden brown and almost set.
*Makes 4 dozen.*

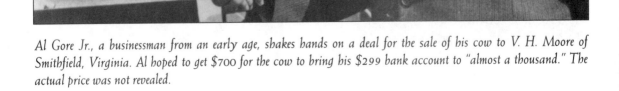

*Al Gore Jr., a businessman from an early age, shakes hands on a deal for the sale of his cow to V. H. Moore of Smithfield, Virginia. Al hoped to get $700 for the cow to bring his $299 bank account to "almost a thousand." The actual price was not revealed.*

## Rosey's Sugar Cookies
*Louise Blackburn*

1 stick margarine or butter, softened to room
  temperature
½ cup sugar
1 egg
½ teaspoon vanilla extract
½ cup vegetable oil
2¼ cups all-purpose flour
½ cup confectioner's sugar
½ teaspoon baking soda
½ teaspoon cream of tartar
Dash of salt

Preheat oven to 375°. Beat together margarine and sugar. Stir in egg, vanilla, and oil. Combine flour, sugar, baking soda, cream of tartar, and salt. Stir into margarine mixture. Chill dough for 1 hour or until easy to handle. Shape dough into 1-inch balls. Place on ungreased cookie sheet. Flatten to ¼-inch with tines of fork, dipping fork in sugar. Bake for 6 to 8 minutes.
*Makes about 40 cookies.*

## Believe-It-or-Not Cookies
*Loren Blair*

1 cup peanut butter
1 cup sugar
1 egg, beaten
1 teaspoon vanilla extract

Preheat oven to 350°. Mix all ingredients well. Drop by the spoonful onto ungreased cookie sheet. Press to form criss-cross designs with fork. Bake for 6 to 7 minutes. Cool and serve.
*Makes 2 dozen.*

## Mama Lucille's Tea Cakes

1 cup sugar
1 cup solid shortening
2 eggs
½ teaspoon lemon extract, if desired
1 teaspoon vanilla extract
½ cup milk
Self-rising flour

Preheat oven to 325°. Mix all ingredients well, using enough flour to make a stiff dough. Chill in refrigerator. Drop dough by spoonfuls onto lightly greased cookie sheet. Bake for 8 to 10 minutes or until lightly browned. Cool and sprinkle confectioner's sugar or granulated sugar over cookies, if desired.
*Makes 2 to 3 dozen.*

## Mama's Brownies
*Cissy Haggard*

1 stick butter
2 cups chocolate chips
¾ cup sugar
2 tablespoons water
1 teaspoon vanilla extract
2 eggs, beaten
1 cup all-purpose flour

Preheat oven to 350°. Melt butter and 1 cup chocolate chips in pan. Add sugar, vanilla, water, eggs, and flour. Mix well. Add 1 cup of chocolate chips. Stir; and pour into baking pan. Bake for 30 minutes. *Optional:* When done, sprinkle with confectioner's sugar.
*Makes 8 to 10 servings.*

*Congressional candidate Al Gore Jr. makes his pitch for these farmers' votes.*

# Rich Mocha Brownies
*Jean Donoho*

4 ounces unsweetened chocolate squares
1½ sticks butter
2 tablespoons instant espresso powder
3 eggs
2 cups sugar
1 cup all-purpose flour
¼ teaspoon salt
1 cup chopped pecans
¼ cup confectioner's sugar
    (add more if needed)
2 tablespoons Kahlua

Preheat oven to 350°. Line a 9x12-inch pan. Combine chocolate and butter in a saucepan. Melt over low heat. Stir until smooth. Stir in espresso powder and set aside to cool. In mixing bowl, beat eggs and sugar until smooth. Add flour and salt. Beat well. Add pecans. Spoon batter into prepared pan. Bake for 35 to 40 minutes. Cool in pan. Whisk together confectioner's sugar and Kahlua until smooth. Spread glaze over brownies. *Makes about 2 dozen.*

# Saucepan Brownies
*Irene Dirkson*

2 sticks butter
1 cup cocoa
2 cups sugar
1½ cups all-purpose flour
3 teaspoons vanilla extract
4 eggs

Preheat oven to 350°. Melt butter and cocoa in saucepan. Remove from heat and add all ingredients, except eggs. Mix. Add eggs and beat well. Pour into a greased 8-inch pan. Bake for 30 minutes.
*Makes 32 small brownies.*

# Tipper Gore's Tennessee Treats

*Nelle Whitehead*

2 cups firmly packed dark brown sugar
2 whole eggs
2 egg whites
2 tablespoons honey
1 teaspoon baking powder, dissolved in ¼ cup boiling water
2 cups all-purpose flour
½ teaspoon cinnamon
⅛ teaspoon allspice
⅛ teaspoon cloves
½ teaspoon salt
½ cup raisins
½ cup chopped dates
½ cup walnut pieces

Preheat oven to 350°. In a large mixing bowl, mix brown sugar and eggs. Add honey and stir. Add baking powder to water and mix. Add to mixture. Combine flour and spices and stir into mixture. Add remaining ingredients and stir. Pour into a greased 8x12-inch baking pan. Bake for 30 to 40 minutes or until a tester inserted in center comes out clean. Cut into squares when warm.

*Note:* This recipe is Tipper Gore's, but it was supplied by Nelle Whitehead, who says that she adds candied cherries and candied pineapple at Christmas, and it is very good. If you leave out the nuts, it is very low fat. Be sure not to overbake. They are better soft.
*Makes about 2 dozen.*

# Bar Chocolate Chip Cookies
*Nelle Whitehead*

⅔ cup solid shortening
⅔ cup butter
1 cup sugar
1 cup firmly packed brown sugar
3 cups self-rising flour
2 eggs
2 teaspoons vanilla extract
6 ounces chocolate chips

Preheat oven to 350°. Mix in order given. Pat into a large greased cake or jellyroll pan. Bake for 20 to 25 minutes. (You can use any flavor chips you like.)

**Frosting**
6 tablespoons margarine
6 tablespoons milk
1⅓ cups sugar
6 ounces chocolate chips

Combine margarine, milk, and sugar in saucepan. Boil for just one minute; remove from heat and add chocolate chips. Beat until thickened to spreading consistency. Spread it over the cookies while still hot.
*Makes 3 dozen.*

## Dump Bars
*Carol Webster*

2 cups sugar
½ cup cocoa
1¾ cups all-purpose flour
1 teaspoon salt
1 cup vegetable oil
1 teaspoon vanilla extract
2 cups chocolate chips, divided
2 cups walnuts, divided

Preheat oven to 350°. Combine first 7 ingredients in bowl; mix well with spoon. Stir in 1 cup chocolate chips and 1 cup walnuts. Pour into a greased 9x13-inch baking pan. Sprinkle 1 cup chocolate chips and 1 cup walnuts over top. Bake for 30 minutes. Makes its own icing while baking. Cut into bars while warm.
*Makes 2 dozen.*

## Raisin Bars
*Roberta Williams*

1½ cups all-purpose flour
1 teaspoon baking powder
1 cup firmly packed brown sugar
1½ cups quick-cooking oats
1½ sticks butter, softened to room
    temperature
2 cups raisins
1½ cups hot water
2 teaspoons cinnamon
½ teaspoon cloves
1 teaspoon vinegar
1 tablespoon butter

Preheat oven to 350°. Combine first 5 ingredients to make a crumbly mixture. Sprinkle ⅔ of this mixture into the bottom of a greased 9x13-inch pan. In a mixing bowl, combine remaining ingredients. Spread over crumb mixture in pan. Cover with remaining crumbs. Bake for 35 minutes. Cook and cut into small squares.
*Makes about 3½ dozen bars.*

## Coffee Party Spice Bars
*Julia Silcox*

¼ cup solid shortening
1 cup firmly packed light brown sugar
1 egg
½ cup hot coffee
1½ cups sifted all-purpose flour
¼ teaspoon salt
1 teaspoon baking powder
¼ teaspoon baking soda
1 teaspoon cinnamon
½ cup raisins
¼ cup chopped walnuts

Preheat oven to 350°. Cream shortening with brown sugar and egg. Stir coffee and flour into this mixture. Sift together salt, soda, baking powder, and cinnamon and combine with other ingredients. Add raisins and chopped nuts; blend well. Place in a greased and floured 9x13-inch pan. Bake for 15 to 20 minutes. Cut into squares and serve. Sprinkle with confectioner's sugar or a thin cream icing, if desired.
*Makes 2 dozen bars.*

# Annual Events in and around Carthage

You're always welcome in Carthage! Here are some favorite annual events that would be excellent times for you and your family to come by for a visit and join in the fun . . . and food.

### May
Classic Car Show on the Bank of the
Cumberland River

Defeated Creek Auto Jam
at the Defeated Creek Marina

### June
Fun Day & Train Excursion at
Gordonsville

Defeated Creek Bluegrass Festival

Civitan Horse Show in Carthage

Junker's Day and town yard sale in Hickman

### October
Cruzin' The Cumberland, from Carthage

Smith County Fall Heritage Festival
in Carthage

### November
Smith County Holiday Open House

Carthage Christmas Parade

### December
Gordonsville Christmas Parade

"Santa Land" in Pleasant Shade

For exact dates, times, and locations, call or write to the Smith County Chamber of Commerce, 130 Third Avenue West, Carthage, TN 37030; (615) 735-2093.

## Nutty Cheese Bars
*Melinda Dennis*

1 18½-ounce butter recipe cake mix
¾ cup butter or margarine, melted
1½ cups chopped pecans or walnuts, divided
1 cup firmly packed brown sugar
2 8-ounce packages cream cheese, softened
    to room temperature

Preheat oven to 350°. Grease and flour a 9x13-inch baking pan. Stir together dry cake mix, melted butter, and ¾ cup chopped pecans until well mixed. Press mixture evenly into the bottom of prepared pan. In a medium bowl, stir brown sugar and cream cheese with a spoon until well mixed. Spread topping evenly over the mixture in the pan. Sprinkle with remaining chopped pecans.

Bake for 25 to 30 minutes or until edges are browned and cheese topping is set. Cool completely before cutting into bars. Store in refrigerator in an airtight container.
*Makes 2 dozen.*

## Peanut Butter Bars
*Thomas Smith*

1 cup firmly packed brown sugar
2 tablespoons peanut butter
2 sticks margarine
2 cups all-purpose flour
½ teaspoon salt
1 teaspoon baking soda
1 cup oats
1 12-ounce package chocolate chips

Preheat oven to 325°. Blend first 7 ingredients together (works best if you mix with your hand), then spread onto an ungreased cookie sheet. Make sure it's as flat as possible. Bake for 25 minutes.

*Frosting:* Shake 1 12-ounce package chocolate chips out evenly across the surface.

Return to the oven for a few minutes to melt the chips. Remove and spread chips around with a table knife. Cool; cut into bars.
*Makes 2 dozen.*

## Peanut Brittle

2 cups sugar
1 cup white corn syrup
½ cup water
½ stick butter or margarine
4 cups raw peanuts
1 teaspoon baking soda

Blend sugar, corn syrup, water, and butter in saucepan. Cook to 230°. Add peanuts and cook to 280°. Stir constantly and continue to cook to 305°. Remove from heat; add baking soda and stir quickly until mixture foams. Quickly pour into 2 buttered 15x10x1-inch pans. Spread thinly over entire surface of pans. Cool until hard and break into pieces.
*Makes about 2 pounds.*

# Roasted Pecan Clusters

3 tablespoons butter or margarine
3 cups pecan pieces
12 ounces (6 squares) chocolate or almond
  bark

Preheat oven to 300°. Melt butter in a
15x10x1-inch jellyroll pan. Spread pecans
evenly in pan. Bake for 30 minutes, stirring
every 10 minutes. Melt bark squares in top of
a double boiler over simmering water; remove
from heat and stir until smooth. Cool 2
minutes. Add pecans and stir until well
coated. Drop by rounded spoonfuls onto wax
paper. Cool completely.
*Makes about 3½ dozen.*

# Caramel Corn

2 cups firmly packed brown sugar
2 sticks butter or margarine
½ cup white corn syrup
1 teaspoon salt
½ teaspoon baking soda
1 teaspoon butter extract
½ teaspoon burnt sugar extract
16 cups popped corn

Preheat oven to 250°. Combine brown sugar,
butter, corn syrup, and salt. Boil for 5 minutes.
Remove from heat. Stir in baking soda and
flavorings. Pour immediately over popcorn.
Put on 1 or 2 large baking pans. Bake for 1
hour, stirring about every 15 minutes. Cool.
Keeps well in tight containers.
*Makes about 8 quarts.*

# Peanut Butter Fudge
*Willa Martin*

2 sticks butter
1 cup peanut butter plus
2 tablespoons peanut butter
3½ cups confectioner's sugar
1 tablespoon vanilla extract
3 tablespoons cocoa

In saucepan, on low heat, melt butter and
peanut butter. Remove from heat. Add
confectioner's sugar, cocoa, and vanilla. Mix
well; pour into an 8-inch pan. Chill in refrigerator. Cut into small squares.
*Makes about 3 dozen.*

# Chocolate-Dipped Strawberries

2 dozen large, unblemished (preferably tart)
  strawberries (caps left on)
2 ounces (2 squares) semisweet chocolate,
  melted according to package directions

Cover a baking sheet or tray with foil or
wax paper. Wash berries quickly in cool
running water or brush them gently with a
damp pastry brush to clean. Dry gently but
thoroughly.

Stir chocolate until smooth. Holding
berries by the cap end, dip one at a time into
the chocolate, coating about ⅔ of the way up
the berry. Scrape excess chocolate from the
tip on the edge of the pan. Place coated
berries on baking sheet.

When all berries are dipped, refrigerate for
at least 15 minutes to harden the chocolate.
Berries will keep in the refrigerator for 24
hours.
*Makes 2 dozen.*

When Al Gore Jr. announced his candidacy for President of the United States, he did it in Carthage, Tennessee. Crowds excited to see Gore and filled the streets to overflowing. Flags were waving, people were cheering. It was an all-American day not soon to be forgotten in Smith County.

Eight years earlier, when Al Gore was running for vice president with Bill Clinton, they campaigned in Carthage.

# Easy Peach Fried Pies

¾ cup sugar
3 tablespoons cornstarch
¾ cup water
3 peaches, peeled and diced
¼ teaspoon almond extract
1 can flaky biscuits (10)
Vegetable oil

Combine first 3 ingredients in a small saucepan; mix well. Cook over low heat, stirring constantly, until smooth and thickened. Remove from heat; stir in peaches and almond extract. Set mixture aside.

Roll each biscuit out on a lightly floured surface to ⅛-inch thickness. Spoon about ¼ cup peach mixture on half of each dough circle. To seal pies, moisten edges of circles and fold in half, making sure edges are even. Using a fork dipped in flour, firmly press dough edges together.

Cook pies in 1-inch deep hot oil (360°) until golden, turning once. Drain on paper towels. Serve warm.
*Makes 10 pies.*

# Mama's Apple Crisp

4 cups sliced pared baking apples
⅔ to ¾ cup firmly packed brown sugar
½ cup all-purpose flour
½ cup oats
¾ teaspoon cinnamon
¾ teaspoon nutmeg
⅓ cup margarine, softened to room temperature

Preheat oven to 350°. Grease baking pan. Arrange apples in pan and mix remaining ingredients with fork. Sprinkle over apples. Bake until apples are tender and topping is brown, about 30 minutes. Serve with ice cream, if desired.
*Makes 6 servings.*

# Quick Peach Dessert

4½ cups sliced fresh peaches
½ cup sugar
1 stick butter or margarine, softened to room temperature
½ cup sugar
1 cup self-rising flour
1 egg, beaten
1 teaspoon vanilla extract

Preheat oven to 350°. Place peaches in a lightly greased 8-inch square baking dish. Sprinkle with ½ cup sugar.

Cream butter and ½ cup sugar, beating well. Add self-rising flour and egg; mix well. Stir in vanilla extract. Spoon mixture over sugared peaches. Bake for 30 to 35 minutes or until golden brown.
*Makes 6 servings.*

# Gooey Cheese Dessert
*Mary Wade Phillips*

½ pint whipping cream, whipped
3 tablespoons sugar
Juice from pineapple plus water to
    make 2 cups liquid
1 3-ounce package strawberry gelatin
24 large marshmallows
1 8-ounce package cream cheese,
    softened to room temperature
1 8¼-ounce can crushed pineapple drained
1 8-ounce carton cottage cheese
1 cup grated American cheese
1 3½-ounce can coconut

Whip the cream and sweeten with sugar; set aside. Heat pineapple juice and water to boiling. Add gelatin, marshmallows, and softened cream cheese, stirring constantly until melted. Cool in refrigerator until partially set. When cool, add drained pineapple, cottage cheese, grated cheese, and coconut. Fold in whipped cream. Chill until firm.
*Makes 8 to 10 servings.*

# Chocolate Peanut Butter Pizza
*Nelle Whitehead*

½ cup sugar
½ cup firmly packed brown sugar
1 stick margarine or butter, softened to room
    temperature
½ cup peanut butter
½ teaspoon vanilla extract
1 egg, beaten
1½ cups all-purpose flour

2 cups miniature marshmallows
1 6-ounce bag of chocolate chips or flavor of
    choice
½ cup chopped pecans, if desired

Preheat oven to 375°. In a large mixing bowl, combine sugar, brown sugar, margarine, peanut butter, vanilla, and egg; blend well. Lightly spoon flour into measuring cup; level off. Stir in flour. Press dough evenly over bottom of 12- or 14-inch pizza pan, forming rim around edge. Bake for 10 minutes. Sprinkle with marshmallows and chocolate chips; continue to bake for 5 to 8 minutes or until marshmallows are puffy and lightly browned. Cool; cut into wedges. Store in tightly covered container.

# Strawberry Pretzel
*Montine Smith*

2 cups pretzels
1½ sticks margarine, melted
3 tablespoons sugar
1 8-ounce package cream cheese, softened to
    room temperature
1 cup sugar
6 ounces whipped topping
1 3-ounce box strawberry gelatin
2 cups boiling water
2 10-ounce packages frozen pretzels

Preheat oven to 375°. Crush pretzels. Mix with margarine and 3 tablespoons sugar. Press into glass dish. Bake for 6 minutes. Cool. Blend cream cheese and sugar. Fold in whipped topping. Spread over pretzel crust. Refrigerate about 10 to 15 minutes. Add gelatin to boiling water. Add strawberries. Chill to syrupy stage. Pour over cheese mixture. Refrigerate for at least 1 hour.
*Makes 6 to 8 servings.*

# Vanilla Ice Cream

2 tablespoons cornstarch
2 quarts milk, divided
4 eggs, separated
2 cups sugar
½ teaspoon salt
2 teaspoons vanilla extract
  (can add more if desired)
1 pint whipping cream

Dissolve cornstarch in 1 cup milk. Heat remaining milk and add cornstarch mixture, stirring constantly. Add well-beaten egg yolks and sugar. Stir constantly and cook over low heat until mixture coats metal spoon. Cool several hours or overnight in refrigerator, if possible.

When ready to freeze, beat egg whites, salt, and vanilla to a froth and add to chilled mixture in 5-quart freezer container. Follow manufacturer's directions for freezing.
*Makes 1 gallon.*

# Homemade Chocolate Ice Cream
*Sharon Raines*

2 cups sugar
3 tablespoons cocoa
2 tablespoons all-purpose flour
10 eggs
1 gallon milk
Ice cream salt

Mix together sugar, cocoa, and flour. Beat eggs and blend into sugar mixture. Pour into freezer bucket. Add enough milk to fill to line on bucket. Follow manufacturer's directions for freezing. It should be firm without melting easily.
*Makes about 1 gallon.*

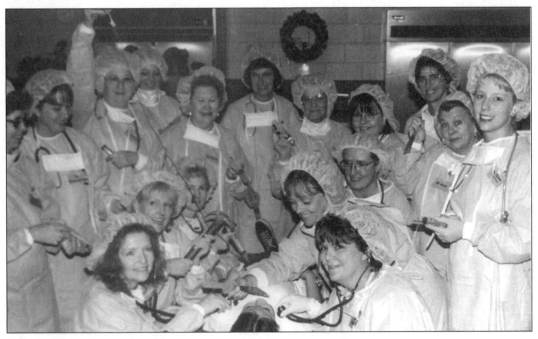

*The teachers and staff at New Middleton Elementary School all dressed alike for their annual Halloween celebration at the school. No one dared to get sick that day!*

# Butter Pecan Ice Cream

2 tablespoons butter or margarine
¼ to ½ cup chopped pecans
1 14-ounce can sweetened condensed milk
  (not evaporated milk)
2 egg yolks, beaten
1 teaspoon maple extract
2 cups heavy cream, whipped

In small saucepan, melt butter; stir in pecans and place in large bowl. Stir in sweetened condensed milk, egg yolks, and maple flavoring. Fold in whipped cream. Pour into foil-lined 9x5-inch loaf pan or other 2-quart container. Cover; freeze for 6 hours or until firm. Scoop ice cream from pan or remove from pan, peel off foil, and slice. Garnish with additional chopped pecans, if desired.
*Makes about 1 quart.*

# Black Walnut Ice Cream

8 egg yolks
1¼ cups sugar
Dash of salt
2 cups milk
2 cups whipping cream
2 teaspoons black walnut flavoring
1 cup chopped black walnuts

Beat egg yolks with sugar until creamy; add salt. Bring milk and cream almost to boiling; remove from heat and pour slowly into egg mixture, stirring constantly.

Return to low heat, stirring constantly to avoid scorching, but do not boil. Add black walnut flavoring. Heat to scalding. Pour mixture into a 1-gallon freezer container. Follow the manufacturer's directions for freezing. When dasher is removed, add black walnuts, stirring to distribute evenly. Pack as freezing instructions direct and allow to "ripen" at least 3 hours before serving.
*Makes 1½ quarts.*

# Sugarless Ice Cream
### Ernestine Bennett

3 12-ounce cans diet orange cola
1 14-ounce can evaporated milk
1 large banana, crushed
1 8-ounce can crushed pineapple, no sugar

Mix all ingredients together. Freeze in ice cream freezer following manufacturer's directions. Serve immediately. (Does not keep well.)
*Makes about 1 quart.*

# Oreo Ice Cream
### Latasha Brown

3 egg yolks
1 14-ounce can condensed milk
4 teaspoons vanilla extract
1 cup or about 12 Oreo cookies, crushed
2 cups whipping cream

In a large bowl, beat egg yolks. Stir in milk and vanilla. Fold in cookies and whipping cream. Pour into a 2-quart container. Cover; freeze 6 hours or until firm.
*Makes about 1 quart.*

# Coconut Fried Ice Cream

1 quart vanilla ice cream
2 eggs, beaten
½ teaspoon vanilla extract
4 cups coconut-flavored cookie crumbs
½ cup flaked coconut

Place 8 scoops of ice cream on a cookie sheet; freeze at least 1 hour or until firm.

Combine eggs and vanilla; mix well and divide in half. Cover half of egg mixture and chill. Combine cookie crumbs and coconut; divide mixture in half. Set half of crumb mixture aside.

Dip each ice cream ball in egg mixture and dredge in crumb mixture. Place on cookie sheet and freeze at least 1 hour or until firm. Remove from freezer; dip in remaining egg mixture and dredge in remaining crumb mixture. Return to cookie sheet; cover and freeze several hours or until firm. Fry ice cream balls in deep hot oil (375°) for 30 seconds or until golden brown. Drain on paper towels and serve immediately.

*Makes 8 servings.*

# Jubilee Rice Pudding
### Lucille Stewart

*Here is a recipe whose name is perfect
for Sunday dessert.*

3 cups milk
3 cups sugar
3 cups cooked rice
1 tablespoon butter
¼ teaspoon salt
2 eggs, beaten
½ cup seedless golden raisins

1 teaspoon pure vanilla extract
½ cup drained, crushed pineapple
⅔ cup strawberry (or your choice) preserves
½ cup chopped pecans or almonds

Combine milk, sugar, rice, butter, and salt in saucepan. Cook over low heat until creamy. Stir pudding mixture into eggs (a little at a time so it won't curdle). Add raisins; stir constantly for about 2 to 3 minutes. Stir in vanilla and pineapple; spoon into 1½-quart mold. Cool. Remove from mold and serve with melted preserves and nuts on top.

# Cream Cheese Mints
### Linda Lankford

1 8-ounce package cream cheese, softened to room temperature
2 tablespoons half-and-half
½ stick soft butter
1 15-ounce package creamy white frosting mix
1 teaspoon peppermint extract
Food coloring as desired

Combine cream cheese, half-and-half, and butter in a heavy-bottomed saucepan. Stir over low heat until cheese mixture is soft, creamy, and butter is melted. Blend in the frosting mix and stir to blend well. Add peppermint extract and food coloring of your choice. You may divide the whole batch to make 2 to 3 different colors. Roll mixture into balls and drop by the spoonful onto wax paper-lined cookie sheet. Press with fork or stamp with cookie stamp. Let mints stand uncovered, at room temperature, until firm and outside is dry.

*Makes 3 to 4 dozen.*

*Celebrations are a regular occurrence in Smith County. Come on over and dance to the music!*

# Lemon Sauce

½ cup sugar
2 tablespoons cornstarch
⅛ teaspoon salt
1 cup water
2 tablespoons grated lemon rind
⅓ cup lemon juice
1 tablespoon butter or margarine

Combine first 4 ingredients in a small saucepan, stirring until smooth. Cook over medium heat, stirring constantly, until smooth and thickened. Add remaining ingredients; cook until thoroughly heated. Serve warm over cake or date nut bread.
*Makes about 1½ cups.*

# Praline Ice Cream Sauce

1½ cups chopped pecans
¼ cup butter or margarine
1¼ cups firmly packed light brown sugar
¾ cup light corn syrup
3 tablespoons all-purpose flour
1 5⅓-ounce can evaporated milk

Preheat oven to 300°. Spread pecans on a baking sheet; bake for 15 minutes. Set aside. Melt butter in a medium saucepan; add sugar, corn syrup, and flour, stirring well. Bring to a boil; reduce heat, and simmer, stirring constantly, for 5 minutes. Remove from heat and let cool to lukewarm. Gradually stir in milk and pecans. Serve warm over ice cream.
*Makes 3 cups.*

# Apple Butter

18 large (about 6 pounds) McIntosh or Jonathan
    apples, cored and quartered
1½ quarts apple cider
1 cup firmly packed brown sugar
1 cup sugar
2 teaspoons cinnamon
½ teaspoon cloves
½ teaspoon nutmeg
⅛ teaspoon salt

In large saucepan, cook apples in cider until tender. Press through a sieve or food mill to separate pulp from skins; discard skins. Return pulp to saucepan with cider. Add remaining ingredients and simmer, uncovered, for 4 to 5 hours, stirring occasionally, until desired thickness is reached. Pour hot mixture into hot, sterilized jars, leaving ¼-inch headspace, and seal tightly with metal lids. Process in boiling water bath for 10 minutes.
*Makes about 6 pints.*

# Strawberry-Pineapple Marmalade

1 medium fresh pineapple
1 teaspoon grated orange rind
2½ cups chopped orange sections
7 cups sugar
1½ quarts fresh strawberries, hulled

Remove leaves and stem end from pineapple. Peel pineapple and trim out eyes; remove core. Chop pineapple and measure 2½ cups.

Combine pineapple, orange rind, oranges, and sugar in a large Dutch oven. Bring to a boil; cook over medium-high heat about 15 minutes, stirring until sugar dissolves. Add strawberries and continue to cook about 35 minutes or until mixture registers 221° on candy thermometer; stir frequently. Remove from heat and skim off foam.

Quickly pour marmalade into hot sterilized jars, leaving ¼-inch headspace; cover at once with metal lids and screw on bands. Process in boiling water bath for 10 minutes.
*Makes 7 half-pints.*

# Pineapple-Watermelon Marmalade

4 cups water
8 lemons, juice and grated rind
Rind of ½ large watermelon (about 4 pounds)
2 teaspoons ginger
1 large ripe pineapple, peeled, cored, and diced
8 cups sugar

Combine water, lemons, rinds, juice, and ginger in a large kettle. Bring to a boil and cook 10 minutes. Skim. Add the diced pineapple and sugar. Stir until sugar is dissolved. Bring to boil, reduce heat, and cook slowly 45 minutes. Cool and seal.
*Makes about 3 pints.*

*A peaceful day on the river near Carthage.*

# PIES

Pies must have been invented in the South. We have pecan pie, peanut butter pie, lemon meringue pie. Throw in the berry and fresh fruit pies that come across our kitchen counters, and you have to agree that you've found a little bit of heaven.

Pastry secrets, special ingredients, and unusual touches that have been passed down from one generation to the next are revealed in these recipes. You'll discover Nelle Whitehead's Brown Sugar Pie, lick your lips after a bite of Molly Phillip Goolsby's Banana Split Cream Cheese Pie, and sigh as you lean back after a bowl of Cathy Kemp's Blackberry Cobbler.

And where do the cooks in Carthage show off their pies? At such annual events as the Defeated Bluegrass Festival, the Fun Festival at Gordonsville, and, of course, at church fellowships.

# The Defeated Creek Bluegrass Festival

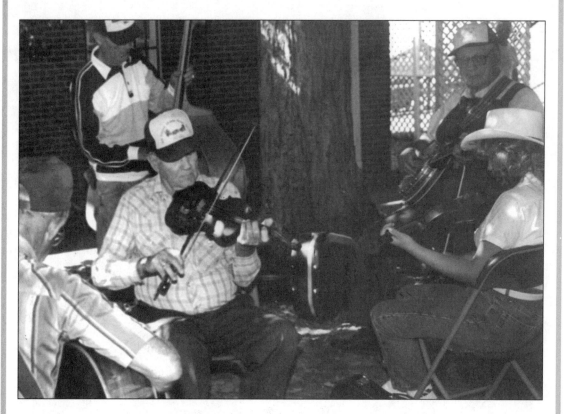

The twang of a flat-top banjo, the thump of an upright bass fiddle, and the acoustic sound of a guitar being strummed invite bluegrass fans to the Defeated Creek Marina in early June. If you love mountain music and dancing, the Defeated Creek Bluegrass Festival is for you. There is a Little Miss Bluegrass Pageant and a dance competition. Perhaps you would rather browse through the craft booths or see the magic shows. You might even try the greased pole climb or the pig chase.

There are also rides and games for kids, an auction, and a raffle. While you're at it, bite down on an ear of corn-on-the-cob, have a piece of Barbara Duff's Pumpkin Apple Pie, or drink down a giant lemonade. And, all the while, everything will be bathed in the great sound of bluegrass music, a sound that echoes comfortably across the mountains and rolling hills of Tennessee.

## Sugarless Apple Pie
*Ernestine Bennett*

1 6-ounce can unsweetened apple juice
2 tablespoons butter, softened
1 teaspoon nutmeg
1½ tablespoons cornstarch
4 sliced yellow apples
2 unbaked 9-inch pie shells

Preheat oven to 350°. In a saucepan, over high heat, bring apple juice to a boil. Add butter, nutmeg, and cornstarch. Set this mixture aside. Place sliced apples in bottom crust. Pour apple juice mixture over apples. This mixture will be a little thick. Do not alter the recipe as cooked apples will make more liquid. Place top crust over apples and seal. Bake for 55 to 60 minutes.
*Makes 6 to 8 servings.*

## Quick Apple Crumb Pie
*Debbie Bush Rich*

1 21-ounce can apple pie filling
1 unbaked 9-inch pie shell
1 stick margarine, melted
1 cup oats
1 cup firmly packed brown sugar
1 cup chopped pecans

Preheat oven to 400°. Place apple pie filling in unbaked pie shell. Mix melted margarine, oats, brown sugar, and pecans. Crumble on top of apples. Bake for 40 to 50 minutes. Top will be golden brown when done. *Note:* The pie shell can be omitted and place ingredients in 9x13-inch glass dish for another type of Apple Crumb.
*Makes 6 to 8 servings.*

## Pumpkin Apple Pie
*Barbara Duff*

⅔ cup firmly packed brown sugar
1 tablespoon cornstarch
½ teaspoon cinnamon
¼ teaspoon salt
⅓ cup water
2 tablespoons butter
3 cups sliced apples
1 egg
⅓ cup sugar
¾ cup canned or cooked mashed pumpkin
¼ teaspoon salt
¼ teaspoon ginger
½ teaspoon cinnamon
⅛ teaspoon cloves
¾ cup evaporated milk

Preheat oven to 375°. Combine brown sugar, cornstarch, ½ teaspoon cinnamon, and ¼ teaspoon salt in a large saucepan. Stir in water and butter. Bring to a boil; add apples and cook 4 minutes over medium heat. Set aside.

Beat eggs in separate bowl. Add sugar, pumpkin, ¼ teaspoon salt, ginger, ½ teaspoon cinnamon, cloves, and evaporated milk. Blend well. Spoon apple mixture into pie shell. Carefully spoon pumpkin layer over apples. Bake for 50 to 55 minutes. If desired, you can garnish with whipped cream and walnut halves.

*Makes 6 to 8 servings.*

## Brown Sugar Pie
*Nelle Whitehead*

2 cups firmly packed brown sugar
2 eggs, beaten
2 tablespoons cornmeal
2 tablespoons cream
1 teaspoon vanilla extract
1 unbaked 9-inch pie shell

Preheat oven to 350°. Cream butter and sugar, add eggs, meal, cream, and vanilla. Pour into uncooked pie shell. Bake for about 45 minutes. This pie is very rich.

*Makes 6 to 8 servings.*

## Buttermilk Pie
*Lucy Hackett-Oldham*

1¼ cups sugar (scant)
2 tablespoons self-rising corn meal mix
3 eggs
7 tablespoons butter or margarine melted
   (Optional: light margarine)
1 teaspoon vanilla extract
1 unbaked 9-inch pie shell
   (Slip this into the oven for about 5 minutes
   before filling or while mixing ingredients;
   this helps to keep the pie from being
   soggy.)

Preheat oven to 350°. Combine sugar and corn meal. Add eggs, melted butter, buttermilk, and vanilla. Blend well. Pour into pie shell. Bake for 40 to 45 minutes or until set. Cool slightly before cutting.

*Makes 6 to 8 servings.*

# From Moonwalking to Bingo

On the first Saturday of each June the Fun Festival is held in Ivy-Agee Memorial Park in Gordonsville. Sponsored by the City of Gordonsville and the Southside Lions Club, this great outdoor festival is jammed with music, food and, just as the name says, fun!

The tempting smell of hot popcorn and swirling cotton candy fills the air. A little girl comes by with a lollipop painted on her cheek and another one in her hand. Children can be heard laughing as they go moonwalking. And someone at the horseshoe stakes shouts with triumph, "It's a ringer!"

Under the elm trees, some of the senior citizens play bingo and dominoes while the younger crowd in the open area run three-legged sack races.

Whatever they're doing, they're having fun. If you want, you can listen and watch live entertainment all day, and then dance all night. But whatever you choose to do, don't choose to miss it!

*Look at those ribs!*

*Tap your toes and clap your hands to the music.*

# No Fuss, No Muss Pie Crust
*Rusty Harding*

1⅓ cups all-purpose flour
1 teaspoon salt *or*
   ½ teaspoon salt and
   ½ teaspoon salt substitute
Milk
Vegetable oil

In a bowl, mix flour and salt. Form a well in the middle. In a one-cup measuring cup, pour ⅓ cup oil. In the same cup, pour in enough milk to fill to 1 cup total liquid.

Pour liquid into the well and mix with a fork until the solids are uniformly dampened, but don't overmix.

Place the ball of dough between 2 sheets of wax paper and roll to the desired size. Remove 1 sheet of wax paper. Pick up the dough by lifting the wax paper and laying it over the rolling pin. Transfer to the pie pan and carefully lift off the other sheet of wax paper. Try not to stretch the dough in the pan. This crust recipe turns out right unless overmixed.
*Makes 1 crust; double the recipe for 2 crusts.*

# Lemon Chess Pie
*O'geal Carter*

2 cups sugar
4 eggs, beaten
1 tablespoon all-purpose flour
1 tablespoon cornmeal
¼ cup milk
¼ cup butter, melted
¼ cup lemon juice
2 teaspoons grated lemon rind
1 unbaked 9-inch pie shell

Preheat oven to 400°. Beat sugar, eggs, flour, and cornmeal in bowl. Add the next 4 ingredients. Mix well. Pour into pie shell. Bake for 10 minutes. Reduce temperature to 300°. Bake for 30 minutes longer or until set.
*Makes 6 to 8 servings.*

# Mrs. Dortha Key's Chess Pie
*Dartha Key*

1 stick butter or margarine, melted
1½ cups sugar
3 eggs, beaten
1 teaspoon vanilla extract
1 teaspoon vinegar
1 teaspoon cornmeal
1 unbaked 9-inch pie shell.

Preheat oven to 300°. Combine first 6 ingredients. Pour into pie shell. Bake at 300° for 10 minutes, then turn heat to 350°. Bake for 30 minutes or until firm.
*Makes 6 to 8 servings.*

# Chocolate Chess Pie
*JoBeth Rich*

1 5⅓-ounce can evaporated milk
1½ cups sugar
3½ tablespoons cocoa
½ stick margarine, melted
2 eggs
1 teaspoon vanilla extract
1 unbaked 9-inch pie shell

Preheat oven to 350°. Combine all ingredients and pour into unbaked pie shell. Bake for 30 to 45 minutes or until set. Test for doneness by shaking gently until it looks firm.
*Makes 6 to 8 servings.*

# Chocolate Swirl Cheese Pie
*Carlise Parham*

1 cup sugar
3 8-ounce packages cream cheese, softened
    to room temperature
5 eggs
1 tablespoon vanilla extract
1 4-ounce package Baker's German sweet
    chocolate, melted and cooled

Preheat oven to 350°. Beat sugar and cheese in a bowl, mixing well. Add eggs, 1 at a time, beating well after each addition. Add vanilla. Measure 2 cups of the cheese mixture; fold in chocolate. Pour remaining cheese mixture into well-buttered 10-inch pie pan or 9-inch square pan. Drop chocolate-cheese mixture by the spoonful on top. Zigzag a spatula through batter to marble. Bake for 40 to 45 minutes. Cool, then chill. Cut into wedges.
*Makes 12 servings.*

# Pineapple Cream Cheese Pie
*Roberta Williams*

1 8-ounce package cream cheese, softened to
    room temperature
1 cup confectioner's sugar
1 16-ounce carton whipped topping
¾ cup drained crushed pineapple
1 9-inch graham cracker pie crust
Graham cracker crumbs

Mix first 3 ingredients until smooth. Add pineapple. Mix well with spoon. Pour into pie shell and top with graham cracker crumbs. Chill for 2 hours.
*Makes 6 to 8 servings.*

# Banana Split Cream Cheese Pie
*Molly Phillips Goolsby*

About 40 vanilla wafers, crushed
½ stick margarine or butter, melted
½ cup pecans, crushed
4 eggs
¾ cup sour cream
2 8-ounce packages cream cheese
2 tablespoons lemon juice
8 ounces whipped topping
Chocolate syrup
Pecans
Pineapple topping
Maraschino cherries

Preheat oven to 300°. Combine first 3 ingredients and press into 9-inch pie pan.
Mix next 4 ingredients and pour into pie shell. Bake for about 45 minutes until it appears firm. Cool.

Place pie on table. Let guests cut their own pie wedges and garnish with their choice of toppings. It is very rich and a little goes a long way.
*Makes 6 to 8 servings.*

*Glenn Duke enjoys sitting in the shade and whittling on a summer day.*

# Tennessee Pear Pie

Pastry for 9-inch double-crust pie
4 large pears, peeled, cored, and thinly sliced
1 cup water
¾ cup sugar
2 tablespoons cornstarch
½ teaspoon nutmeg
½ teaspoon cinnamon
½ teaspoon allspice
2 tablespoons honey
1 tablespoon lemon juice
2 tablespoons butter or margarine, melted
1 tablespoon sugar
Whipped cream
Ground nutmeg

Roll half of pastry to a ⅛-inch thickness on a lightly floured surface; fit into a 9-inch pie plate. Combine pears and water in a saucepan over high heat. Bring water to a boil, reduce heat, and simmer 10 minutes. Drain, reserving ½ cup liquid; set pears and liquid aside.

Preheat oven to 425°. Combine ¾ cup sugar, cornstarch, and spices in a large mixing bowl. Combine reserved pear liquid, honey, and lemon juice; mix well. Stir into sugar mixture. Add cooked pears, stirring well to coat; pour mixture into pastry shell.

Roll out remaining pastry to a ⅛-inch thickness and place over filling. Trim edges; seal and flute. Cut slits to allow steam to escape. Brush top of pie evenly with butter; sprinkle with 1 tablespoon sugar. Bake for 30 to 35 minutes (cover edges with foil to prevent overbrowning, if necessary). Serve warm or cool. Top slices with whipped cream and nutmeg, if desired.
*Makes 6 to 8 servings.*

# Delicious Chocolate Chip Pie
*Judy Hackett*

½ cup self-rising flour
2 teaspoons vanilla extract
1 cup chocolate chips
1 cup chopped pecans
¾ cup sugar
¾ cup firmly packed brown sugar
2 sticks butter, melted
2 eggs, beaten
1 unbaked 9-inch pie shell

Preheat oven to 325°. Combine first 6 ingredients. Mix in eggs and melted butter. Blend well. Pour into pie shell. Bake for 1 hour or until firm.
*Makes 6 to 8 servings.*

# Virgie's Chocolate Pie
*Virgie Mae Bass*

1 cup sugar
1¼ cups milk
3 level tablespoons cocoa
2 tablespoons all-purpose flour
3 eggs (yolks and whites separated)
2 teaspoons butter
1 teaspoon vanilla extract
1 baked 9-inch pie shell
⅓ cup sugar

Preheat oven to 350°. Combine first 7 ingredients in saucepan. Cook until thick. Pour into baked pie shell. Beat the egg whites until soft peaks form. Gently blend in ⅓ cup sugar. Spread pie with meringue. Bake until lightly browned.
*Makes 6 to 8 servings.*

# Here Comes Santa Claus

When the air turns nippy in Middle Tennessee and when the turkey has been eaten, the children want to know, "When's the Christmas parade?"

The annual Carthage Christmas Parade is always on the Sunday after Thanksgiving. And it's a great parade. Where else can you see a giant piggy bank float, a marching grinch, or Santa Scouts? And, of course, all the kids—"from one to ninety-two"—eagerly await the familiar sound of "Ho, ho, ho!" in the distance. Then we stand on tiptoe to catch a glimpse of the jolly fat guy in the bright red suit who's the star of the show.

Actually, people in Carthage get into the holiday mood even earlier than the parade by hosting an old-time holiday open house on the second Sunday in November. Businesses open their doors for special sales, Christmas specials, door prizes, giveaways, and free refreshments, like Christmas cookies and hot apple cider. Everyone strolls down the city sidewalks sipping cider, visiting with shopkeepers, and talking to friends and neighbors. It's one of our favorite days of the year.

Oh, by the way, you can come, too. Everyone's welcome!

*The football float is always a favorite.*

*Santa Scouts wave at their friends and families.*

## Fudge Pie
*Christy Kemp*

1 cup sugar
2 tablespoons all-purpose flour
4 tablespoons cocoa
½ cup milk
2 eggs
3 tablespoons butter, melted
1 teaspoon vanilla extract
1 deep-dish pie shell

Preheat oven to 325°. Combine first 7 ingredients with mixer. Pour into pie shell. Bake for 45 minutes or until firm. Great served warm with whipped cream or ice cream.
*Makes 6 to 8 servings.*

## Mrs. Lowe Smith's Coconut Cream Pie
*Dartha Key*

⅓ cup all-purpose flour
⅔ cup sugar
Pinch of salt
2 cups hot milk
3 egg yolks, beaten
2 tablespoons butter
½ teaspoon vanilla extract
1 cup fresh coconut
1 baked 9-inch pie shell
3 egg whites
¼ teaspoon salt
⅓ cup sugar

Blend flour, sugar, and pinch of salt in saucepan. Add 2 cups hot milk and egg yolks. Cook until thick (about 5 minutes). Add butter and cool. Add vanilla and coconut. Pour into baked pie shell. Preheat oven to 300°. Beat the egg whites until soft peaks form. Gently blend in salt and sugar. Cover pie. Bake until meringue is lightly browned.
*Makes 6 to 8 servings.*

## Old-Fashioned Egg Pie
*Thomas Stewart*

6 egg yolks
2 cups sugar, divided
2 tablespoons all-purpose flour
2 cups milk
Dash of salt
1 teaspoon lemon extract
2 teaspoons vanilla extract

Preheat oven to 400°. Beat yolks with ½ cup sugar and flour. Add remainder of sugar, salt, and milk. Beat well. Add extracts. Place in unbaked pie shell. Bake in 400° oven until top is crusty, then reduce heat to 375° and bake for 25 to 30 more minutes or until firm.
*Makes 2 pies.*

## Apple Cobbler

3 tablespoons brown sugar
¼ teaspoon cinnamon
¼ teaspoon nutmeg
1 teaspoon lemon juice
2 medium cooking apples, peeled, and sliced
⅓ cup all-purpose flour
2 tablespoons sugar
1 teaspoon baking soda
2 tablespoons milk
1 tablespoon vegetable oil

Preheat oven to 375°. Combine sugar, cinnamon, nutmeg, and lemon juice; add apples and toss well to coat. Spoon apple mixture into two 10-ounce custard cups. Set aside.

Combine flour, sugar, and baking powder in a small bowl. Combine milk and oil; stir into flour mixture until moistened. Drop dough by the spoonful onto apple mixture. Bake for 15 to 20 minutes. Serve warm.
*Makes 2 servings.*

# Blackberry Cobbler
*Cathy Kemp*

1 cup all-purpose flour
1 cup sugar
1 teaspoon baking powder
½ cup milk
1 stick butter or margarine, melted
2 cups hot, sweetened blackberries

Melt butter in a 10x6x2-inch glass dish. Mix together flour, sugar, baking powder, milk, and margarine; pour into dish. Cover with hot, sweetened blackberries and stir slightly to mix in blackberries. Bake for 30 minutes.
*Makes 4 servings.*

# Fruit Cobbler
*Maudie Comstock*

1 cup all-purpose flour
1 cup sugar
1 cup milk
1 stick margarine, melted
3 cans fruit, canned or fresh

Preheat oven to 300°. Mix all ingredients, except fruit, and place in a deep baking dish. Pour fruit over top and bake until crust comes to the top and browns.
*Makes 6 to 8 servings.*

# Japanese Fruit Pie
*JoBeth Rich*

1 stick margarine, melted
1 cup sugar
2 eggs
½ cup pecans, cut in halves
½ cup raisins
½ cup coconut
1 tablespoon vinegar
1 unbaked 9-inch pie shell

Preheat oven to 325°. Melt margarine and cool. Add the next 6 ingredients; mix well. Pour into pie shell and bake for 40 minutes.
*Makes 6 servings.*

# Gooey Shoo-Fly Pie
*Rhonda Rush*

2 cups all-purpose flour
¾ cup firmly packed brown sugar
⅓ cup butter or shortening
½ teaspoon nutmeg, optional
1 teaspoon cinnamon, optional
1 cup molasses
½ cup firmly packed brown sugar
2 eggs
1 cup hot water
1 teaspoon soda, dissolved in hot water
2 unbaked 9-inch pie shells

Preheat oven to 400°. Mix together first 5 ingredients until crumbly in a bowl. In another bowl, mix together remaining ingredients. Pour some of the syrup into pie shells, then add ½ of the crumbs. Add the remaining syrup and the rest of the crumbs. Bake for 10 minutes at 400°, then reduce the heat to 350° for 50 minutes.
*Makes 2 pies.*

## Lemon Freeze Pie
*Crelious Sadler*

¾ cup graham cracker crumbs
2 tablespoons sugar
½ stick margarine, melted
2 eggs, separated
1 14-ounce can condensed milk
⅓ cup fresh or bottled lemon juice
3 tablespoons sugar

Combine crumbs (reserving 4 tablespoons), 2 tablespoons sugar, and melted butter; press in bottom of pan. Beat egg yolks; blend in milk and lemon juice. Beat egg whites gradually until peaks form. Beat in 3 tablespoons sugar. Fold into lemon mixture. Pour in crumb-lined pan. Sprinkle crumbs on top and freeze.
*Makes 6 servings.*

## Molasses Pie

2 cups molasses
1 cup sugar
3 eggs
1 tablespoon butter, melted
1 lemon, squeezed
Nutmeg to taste
1 unbaked 9-inch pie shell

Preheat oven to 375°. Mix first 6 ingredients together. Pour into pie shell. Bake for about 45 to 55 minutes or until firm.
*Makes 6 to 8 servings.*

## Caramel Pecan Apple Pie

Pastry for double-crust 9-inch pie
6 cups apples, peeled and thinly sliced
¾ cup sugar
2 tablespoons all-purpose flour
¼ teaspoon salt
2 tablespoons butter or margarine
⅓ cup caramel ice cream topping
2 teaspoons chopped pecans

Preheat oven to 425°. Roll half of pastry onto a lightly floured surface to an ⅛-inch thickness; fit into a 9-inch pie plate. Chill remaining pastry.

Combine apples, sugar, flour, and salt; toss gently to coat. Spoon mixture into pastry shell; dot with butter.

Roll out remaining pastry to an ⅛-inch thickness and place over filling. Trim edges; seal and flute. Cut several slits in top crust. Bake pie for 35 to 40 minutes. Remove from oven; immediately drizzle caramel topping over top. Sprinkle with pecans. Serve warm or at room temperature.
*Makes 6 to 8 servings.*

*Tipper Gore helps with a Democratic fund raiser at Ivy-Agee Memorial Park in Gordonsville.*

# Black Bottom Pecan Pie

¼ cup cornstarch
⅓ cup bourbon
3 eggs
¾ cup sugar
1 stick butter or margarine, melted
½ cup light corn syrup
1 cup chopped pecans
1 6-ounce package semisweet chocolate chips
1 unbaked 9-inch pie shell
Whipped cream

Preheat oven to 350°. In small bowl, combine cornstarch and bourbon; set aside. In large bowl, beat eggs. Add sugar, butter, corn syrup, and bourbon-cornstarch mixture. Stir in pecans and chocolate chips. Pour into pie shell. Bake for 30 to 35 minutes. (Filling should be slightly less set in center of pie than around edges.) Chocolate chips will melt and settle on bottom of pie while it is baking, thus giving the pie its name. Cool and garnish with whipped cream.
*Makes 6 to 8 servings.*

# Pecan Pie
### Sandy Stafford

1 cup sugar
½ cup dark corn syrup
½ cup butter, melted
3 eggs, well beaten
1 cup chopped pecans
1 unbaked 9-inch pie shell

Preheat oven to 400°. Mix sugar, syrup, and butter. Add eggs and pecans. Mix all together well. Bake in a 400° oven for 10 minutes. Reduce heat to 350° and continue baking for 25 to 30 minutes.
*Makes 6 servings.*

# Y'all Come Back Pinto Bean Pie

*Rusty Harding*

½ cup pinto beans, cooked and mashed
  (Leave a few only partially mashed for
  effect, if you wish.)
1½ cups sugar
1 stick margarine, melted
2 large eggs, beaten
1 cup shredded coconut
1 teaspoon apple cider vinegar
1 tablespoon vanilla extract
1 unbaked 9-inch pie shell

Preheat oven to 350°. Combine first 7 ingredients and mix thoroughly. Pour into an uncooked pie shell. Bake for approximately 35 to 45 minutes, or until set or very lightly browned on top. If the crust gets brown before the pie is done, remove the pie from the oven; protect the crust with foil and return to the oven until done.

*Note:* Precooked, canned pinto beans, well drained, make this recipe very fast to make. If you don't have apple cider vinegar, white vinegar can be substituted with only a small change in taste.

*Makes 8 servings.*

# Raisin Cream Meringue Pie

1 4¾-ounce package vanilla pudding mix
1 14-ounce can condensed milk
  (not evaporated milk)
2 cups water
3 eggs, separated
½ teaspoon cinnamon
¼ teaspoon nutmeg
1 cup seedless raisins
1 baked 9-inch pie shell
¼ teaspoon cream of tartar

Preheat oven to 350°. In large heavy saucepan, combine pudding mix, condensed milk, water, egg yolks, cinnamon, and nutmeg; mix well. Over medium heat, cook and stir until thickened. Stir in raisins. Pour into prepared crust. In small mixer bowl, beat egg whites with cream of tartar, beating until soft peaks form; gradually add sugar, beating until stiff but not dry. Spread meringue on top of pie, sealing carefully to edge of shell. Bake for 10 to 15 minutes or until meringue is golden brown. Cool. Chill thoroughly, about 4 hours. Refrigerate leftovers.

*Makes 6 to 8 servings.*

# Grandma Lulu's Sweet Potato Pie
*Lulu King*

2 cups sweet potatoes, peeled, cooked and mashed
3 eggs, well beaten
½ stick butter, softened to room temperature
1 cup sugar
⅛ teaspoon salt
¼ teaspoon nutmeg
½ teaspoon cinnamon
2 tablespoons all-purpose flour
3 tablespoons milk
1 unbaked 9-inch pie shell

Preheat oven to 425°. In large mixing bowl, mix first 9 ingredients together. Pour into pie shell and bake until firm.
*Makes 6 to 8 servings.*

*Lots of visitors come to Carthage and Smith County to shop in the many antique shops.*

# CAKES

Scrumptious eating down to the last crumb. That's the kind of delightful recipes you'll find here as Carthage cooks share their secrets of great cakes. From multi-layered miracles from scratch to boxed cake mixes, these cakes taste as if they came from the world's most famous ovens and will be the perfect finishing touch for your great Southern meal.

Why not give Bonnie McKinney's Swedish Nut Cake a try? Or try your hand at Vickey Fields' Honey Bun Cake. Whichever recipe you decide to make, your guests will be glad you did.

Recipes for great cakes are handed down from mother to daughter to granddaughter. And you find them on the family table at special holiday gatherings year after year, as Betty Moore describes when she tells about the traditions at the lovely old Hull House.

## Swedish Nut Cake
*Mrs. Bonnie McKinney*

2 cups all-purpose flour
2 teaspoons baking soda
1 cup sugar
3 eggs
1 20-ounce can crushed pineapple, drained
2 teaspoons vanilla extract
1 cup chopped nuts

Preheat oven to 350°. Sift flour and add baking soda; set aside. Combine sugar with eggs; add crushed pineapple and vanilla. Add dry ingredients, ½ cup at a time. Stir in nuts and pour into greased and floured bundt pan. Bake for 40 minutes. Cool 5 to 10 minutes before placing on cake rack. Prepare Cream Cheese Icing and frost cake.

### Cream Cheese Icing
2 cups confectioner's sugar
1 8-ounce package cream cheese, softened to room temperature
2 tablespoons milk
1 teaspoon vanilla

Sift sugar into a mixing bowl. Add remaining ingredients, mix until smooth. Spread over Swedish Nut Cake.
*Makes 10 servings.*

## Hot Puddin' Cake and Chocolate Sauce
*A Stewart Family Favorite*

1½ cups sugar
1 stick butter, softened to room temperature
½ teaspoon salt
½ teaspoon baking soda
1½ teaspoons baking powder

2½ cups all-purpose flour
½ cup buttermilk
2 teaspoons vanilla extract
2 eggs

### Chocolate Sauce
½ teaspoon salt
2 cups sugar
2 tablespoons cornstarch
4 tablespoons cocoa
⅓ stick butter
3 cups water
  (or milk if you desire a thicker sauce)
2 teaspoons vanilla extract

Preheat oven to 350°. Cream 1½ cups sugar and butter until smooth. Add ½ teaspoon salt, soda, baking powder, and flour. Mix well. Add buttermilk and 2 teaspoons vanilla, then add eggs. Pour batter in greased iron skillet. Bake for 30 to 35 minutes.

**Chocolate Sauce:** Mix dry ingredients together in a saucepan. Add water/milk, butter, and vanilla. Cook, stirring often, until sauce is thick. Serve sauce hot over cake.
*Makes 10 servings.*

## Skillet Pineapple Upside-Down Cake
*Debra Smith*

½ stick butter or margarine
1 cup firmly packed brown sugar
½ cup chopped pecans
1 15¼-ounce can pineapple slices, undrained
3 eggs, separated
1 cup sugar
1 cup all-purpose flour
1 teaspoon baking powder
1 teaspoon salt
6 or 7 Maraschino cherries

Preheat oven to 375°. Melt butter in a 9-inch cast-iron skillet. Add brown sugar and pecans; mix well. Drain pineapple, reserving ¼ cup plus 1 tablespoon pineapple juice; set juice aside. Arrange pineapple slices in a single layer over brown sugar mixture; set skillet aside.

Beat egg yolks until thick and lemon colored; gradually add sugar, beating well. Combine flour, baking powder, and salt; add to egg mixture. Stir in reserved pineapple juice.

Beat egg whites (at room temperature) until stiff peaks form; fold into flour mixture. Spoon batter evenly over pineapple slices. Bake for 30 to 35 minutes. Immediately invert cake onto a serving plate. Place cherries in centers of pineapple rings.

*Makes 10 servings.*

# Black Walnut Cake
### Wilma Fisher

2 cups sugar
1 cup butter flavored shortening
½ cup cocoa
3 eggs
¼ cup milk
1 teaspoon salt
1 teaspoon baking powder
1 cup all-purpose flour
1 teaspoon black walnut extract
2 teaspoons vanilla extract
1 cup chopped black walnuts
Caramel Frosting (see recipe on Page 165)

Mix sugar, shortening, and cocoa until blended. Add eggs, milk, baking powder, salt, and flour. Mix well. Add extracts and walnuts. Pour into 10x14-inch baking pan. Bake 20 to 25 minutes or until tester inserted in center comes out clean. Do not overbake. Prepare Caramel Frosting and frost cooled cake.

*Makes 10 to 12 servings.*

# Chocolate-Covered Cherry Cake
### Sharon Raines

1 18½-ounce box butter recipe fudge cake mix
3 eggs
1 21-ounce can cherry pie filling
1 teaspoon almond extract
1 stick butter
1 cup sugar
1 cup evaporated milk
1 6-ounce package chocolate chips
1 teaspoon almond extract

Preheat oven to 350°. Combine first 4 ingredients. Pour into 13x9-inch pan. Bake for 25 minutes. Let cool.

Melt butter, add sugar and milk. Bring to a boil and boil for 2 minutes, stirring constantly. Remove from heat and stir in chocolate chips and extract. Beat by hand until thickened a little. Pour over cake.

*Makes 10 to 12 servings.*

Mrs. Inez Owens talks about Al Gore: "Some people say Al will change, but I don't believe it. Al and Tipper are down-to-earth people, and I believe that the reason Al was put on this earth was so he could serve down-to-earth people." Mrs. Inez is a talented cook. Her Old-Fashioned Pound Cake is wonderful!

# Mrs. Inez's Old-Fashioned Pound Cake

*Mrs. Inez Owens*

3 cups sugar
1 cup butter
6 eggs (yolks separated)
1 teaspoon vanilla extract
1 teaspoon lemon extract
3 cups all-purpose flour, sifted with
½ teaspoon salt, and ¼ teaspoon soda
1 cup buttermilk

Preheat oven to 350°. In mixing bowl, cream sugar and butter until light and creamy. Add egg yolks, one at a time, and beat well. Add vanilla and lemon extracts. Add sifted dry ingredients, ¼ cup at a time, alternately with buttermilk. Beat egg whites and fold into mixture. Pour batter into a bundt pan. Bake for 1¼ hours. After cake has cooled, serve with your choice of fresh fruit and whipped cream topping.

# Hull House

$S$ome people have a real knack for making history come alive. Betty Moore is one of those great storytellers. Perhaps her skill comes from living in a house where so much history took place and then restoring it to its original beauty, as Betty and her husband Bill have done with Hull House.

Named for Cordell Hull, who served as Secretary of State under Franklin D. Roosevelt, this wonderful old place was acquired by Bill Moore's grandparents in 1920. In 1976 Bill and Betty inherited it.

The popularity and love the townsfolk have for the 1889 house quickly became known to them when they held an open house their first year there. "*The Carthage Courier* annouced our open house in its Thursday edition, and on Sunday we had five hundred people show up," Betty said.

What was once the largest mansion in Smith County, and surely the most impressively decorated, is once again wearing with pride its original grandeur.

The lovely brick exterior welcomes guests to enjoy the past so attractively presented by the large, high-ceilinged rooms, winding staircase, massive woodwork, and fireplaces throughout the house. A beautiful wardrobe that belonged to Al and Tipper Gore when they were in Nashville graces one of the lovely rooms.

The Moores are generous in sharing their home because of its connection with some of the most important characters in Carthage history and because of its architecture. They often host lawn parties and tours to raise funds for local scholarships.

"This house revolves around food," says Betty when you ask her about family traditions. "We regularly have thirty to fifty people here for holiday dinners, and we've had as many as a hundred come for meals and music."

Betty prepares the basic meats and desserts, and other family members bring the rest. "Until I learned better," she laughs, "I used to have all our friends in for New Year's Eve, and I'd fix everything: blackeyed peas, hog jowl, Mexican cornbread, potatoes."

"We're always going to the excess in this house, maybe because it's so big," she says. "For example, an old cherry tree from the front yard made four sets of furniture!"

Betty's and Bill's hard work, extensive research, and determination paid off again in 1983 when Hull House was finally placed on the National Register of Historic Places. It is not to be missed when you come to Carthage!

# Cinnamon & Sour Cream Pound Cake

*Uvon Spigner*

2 sticks butter or margarine, softened to room
   temperature
2 cups sugar
2 cups all-purpose flour
2 teaspoons baking powder
½ teaspoon salt
8 ounces sour cream
1 teaspoon vanilla extract
½ cup chopped pecans
½ teaspoon cinnamon
2 teaspoons sugar

Preheat oven to 350°. Combine butter and 2
cups sugar. Cream with mixer until light and
fluffy. Add eggs, one at a time, beating 30
seconds after each addition. Combine flour,
baking powder, and salt; stir ⅓ of the flour
mixture into creamed mixture with a spoon
until blended. Add ½ the sour cream to
creamed mixture. Repeat procedure ending
with dry ingredients. Stir in vanilla.

Combine pecans, cinnamon, and 2
teaspoons sugar; sprinkle ⅓ of mixture into a
greased and floured 10-inch bundt pan. Pour
½ the batter into pan; sprinkle ⅓ of nut
mixture over batter. Pour remaining batter
into pan and sprinkle with remaining nut
mixture. Bake for 55 to 60 minutes. Cool 1
hour in pan.
*Makes 10 to 12 servings.*

# Buttermilk Pound Cake

2 sticks butter, softened to room temperature
2 cups sugar
4 eggs
3 cups all-purpose flour
½ teaspoon baking soda
¼ teaspoon salt
1 cup buttermilk
1 teaspoon vanilla extract
1 teaspoon lemon extract

Preheat oven to 325°. Cream butter; gradually
add sugar, beating at medium speed of an
electric mixer until well blended. Add eggs,
one at a time, beating after each addition.

Combine flour, soda, and salt; add to
creamed mixture alternately with buttermilk,
beginning and ending with flour mixture. Stir
in extracts. Pour batter into a greased and
floured 10-inch tube pan. Bake for 1 hour or
until a tester inserted in center comes out
clean. Cool in pan 10 minutes; remove from
pan and cool completely on a rack.
*Makes 10 to 12 servings.*

# Chocolate Punch Bowl Cake

*Dolores Silcox Bowman*

1 18½-ounce box German chocolate cake mix
12 ounces cream cheese, softened to room
   temperature
½ box confectioner's sugar
16 ounces whipped topping
1 12-ounce bottle chocolate syrup
1 3-ounce box instant chocolate pudding
4 Heath Bars, crumbled

Preheat oven to 350°. Prepare cake mix according to directions. Bake cake, then cool and cut into 2-inch squares. Prepare pudding according to directions. Mix cream cheese, sugar, and whipped topping together. In a punch bowl, place enough cake squares to cover the bottom. Add a layer of chocolate syrup, cream cheese mixture, then pudding. Sprinkle 1 Heath Bar on top. Repeat these steps until all ingredients are gone. This cake should make 3 layers in the punch bowl. Refrigerate for at least 2 hours before serving.
*Makes 12 to 16 servings.*

# Lemon Picnic Cake

*Aldoria Valentine*

1 18½-ounce box yellow cake mix
½ cup vegetable oil
¾ cup water
1 3½-ounce package instant lemon pudding
   mix
4 eggs
2 cups confectioner's sugar
⅓ cup orange juice
2 tablespoons butter, melted
2 tablespoons water

Preheat oven to 350°. Combine cake mix, oil, water, and pudding mix and beat for 2 minutes. Add eggs, 1 at a time, and beat well. Bake in a greased and floured 9x13-inch pan for 35 minutes or until a tester inserted in center comes out clean. While cake is baking, combine remaining ingredients to make the glaze. Mix well. While cake is hot, prick entire top with a toothpick. Pour glaze over top.
*Makes 10 to 12 servings.*

# Sorghum Cake

¾ cup solid shortening
¾ cup sugar
2 eggs
1 cup chunky applesauce
1 cup sorghum syrup
2½ cups all-purpose flour
1½ teaspoons baking soda
1 teaspoon salt
1 teaspoon cinnamon
½ teaspoon cloves
½ teaspoon nutmeg

Preheat oven to 350°. Cream shortening and sugar until light and fluffy. Add eggs, one at a time, beating after each addition. Add applesauce and sorghum syrup; beat well.

Combine flour, soda, salt, cinnamon, cloves, and nutmeg; stir into batter. Pour batter into 3 greased and floured 8-inch round cake pans.

Bake for 20 to 25 minutes or until a tester inserted in center comes out clean. Cool in pans 10 minutes. Remove layers from pans; cool completely on wire racks. Frost with desired frosting between layers and on top of cake.
*Makes 10 to 12 servings.*

## Dried Apple Stack Cake

½ cup solid shortening
½ cup sugar
½ cup molasses
½ cup buttermilk
1 egg, beaten
1 teaspoon vanilla extract
3 to 3½ cups all-purpose flour
1 teaspoon ginger
½ teaspoon baking soda
½ teaspoon salt
4 cups dried apple slices
3½ cups water
1½ cups sugar
½ teaspoon cinnamon
½ teaspoon nutmeg

Preheat oven to 350°. Cream shortening; gradually add sugar and molasses, beating until smooth. Add buttermilk, egg, and vanilla; mix well. Combine flour, ginger, soda, and salt. Gradually add to creamed mixture, beating just until blended.

Divide dough into 6 portions and pat 1 portion into the bottom of a lightly greased, 9-inch cast-iron skillet. (Chill remaining dough.) Bake for 8 to 9 minutes. Carefully remove to cooling rack. Repeat with remaining dough. Set layers aside.

Combine apples and water in a large saucepan. Bring to a boil; cover, reduce heat, and simmer 30 minutes or until tender. Stir in sugar and spices.

Stack layers, spreading apple filling between each. Store overnight in refrigerator before serving.
*Makes 8 to 10 servings.*

## Rum Cake
*Mrs. Dillard*

½ cup chopped pecans
1 18½-ounce package yellow cake mix
1 3¾-ounce package instant vanilla pudding mix
½ cup dark rum (any kind)
½ cup water
½ cup vegetable oil
4 eggs, beaten

Preheat oven to 325°. Grease and flour a 10-inch tube cake pan or bundt pan. Sprinkle nuts in bottom of pan. Combine remaining ingredients; mix well. Pour batter into pan. Bake for 1 hour.

**Hot Rum Glaze**
1 cup sugar
1 stick margarine
¼ cup water
¼ cup rum

Combine all ingredients; boil for 2 to 3 minutes. Pour over hot cake.
*Makes 10 to 12 servings.*

## Honey Bun Cake
*Vickey Fields*

1 18½-ounce box yellow cake mix
4 eggs
¾ cup vegetable oil
8 ounces sour cream
1 cup brown sugar
1 tablespoon cinnamon
1½ cups powdered sugar
6 tablespoons milk
1 tablespoon vanilla extract

Preheat oven to 350°. Mix together the first 4 ingredients. Pour half the batter into a 9x13-inch cake pan. Combine brown sugar and cinnamon and spread over the first layer of batter. Pour on remaining batter. Cook for 1 hour or until a tester inserted in center comes out clean. Combine remaining ingredients for topping. Poke holes in cake with skewer. While hot, pour topping over cake. Let stand for 1 to 2 hours.
*Makes 10 to 12 servings.*

## Preacher's Cake
*Lorie Blair*

2 cups sugar
2 cups all-purpose flour
1 teaspoon baking soda
½ teaspoon salt
2 eggs
2 teaspoons vanilla extract
½ cup chopped nuts
1 20-ounce can crushed pineapple

Preheat oven to 350°. Combine first 4 ingredients; add remaining ingredients and mix by hand. Pour into a greased and floured 9x13-inch pan. Bake for 45 minutes.

**Cream Cheese Frosting**
1 8-ounce package cream cheese, softened to
   room temperature
1¾ cups confectioner's sugar
½ stick butter, softened to room temperature
¼ teaspoon salt
½ cup chopped nuts
2 teaspoons vanilla extract

Mix all ingredients well. Spread over cooled cake.
*Makes 10 to 12 servings.*

## Sugarless Cake
*Mary Harris*

1 stick butter, melted
2 eggs
1 tablespoon liquid sweetener
1½ cups no-sugar applesauce
3 medium bananas, mashed
½ cup chopped dates or raisins
½ teaspoon cinnamon
¼ teaspoon allspice
1 teaspoon vanilla extract
2 cups all-purpose flour
2 teaspoons baking soda
1 cup chopped pecans

Preheat oven to 400°. Mix all ingredients well. Grease and flour a 10-inch tube pan. Pour batter into pan. Bake for 40 minutes.
*Makes 10 to 12 servings.*

## Five-Flavor Cake
*Irene Dirkson*

1 18½-ounce box yellow cake mix
1½ cups self-rising flour
⅔ cup sugar
1 teaspoon vanilla extract
1 teaspoon lemon extract
1 teaspoon rum extract
1 teaspoon pineapple extract
1 teaspoon orange extract

Preheat oven to 350°. Mix cake mix as directed on box. Blend in remaining ingredients. Beat well with mixer. Bake in a greased and floured 10-inch tube pan or bake in layered pans. Bake 30 to 40 minutes or until a tester inserted in center comes out clean. May frost with frosting of your choice.
*Makes 10 to 12 servings.*

*The Carthage United Methodist Church building was completed in 1889 and shows a fine example of late nineteenth century vernacular Gothic Revivial Church architecture. A collection of stained-glass windows dates back to the nineteenth century with the oldest window being installed when the building was erected in 1889. On September 4, 1985, this wonderful old building was placed on the National Register of Historic Places.*

# Jam Cake
*Nelle Whitehead*

1 cup margarine or shortening
2 cups sugar
1 cup buttermilk
6 eggs, beaten
2 teaspoons baking soda
1 teaspoon cloves
1 teaspoon nutmeg
1 teaspoon cinnamon
1 teaspoon allspice
3 cups all-purpose flour
1 pound chopped black walnuts or pecans
  (or less)
2 cups blackberry or strawberry jam
1 16-ounce can whole cooked cranberry
  sauce

Preheat oven to 350°. Cream together first 3 ingredients. Mix in remaining ingredients, blending well. Pour into three 9-inch greased and floured layer cake pans (or 4 8-inch pans.) Bake for 30 minutes or until tester inserted in center comes out clean. Frost with Caramel Frosting.

**Caramel Frosting**
⅔ cup milk
1 cup margarine or butter
2 cups firmly packed brown sugar
1 16-ounce box confectioner's sugar

Combine milk, butter, and brown sugar in saucepan. Boil 3 minutes and add confectioner's sugar. Beat until hard enough to spread. Decorate with pecan halves or candied cherries at Christmas.
*Makes 10 to 12 servings.*

# Aunt Henrietta's Holiday Jam Cake
*Henrietta Carver*

1 cup solid shortening, margarine or butter
2 cups sugar
6 whole eggs
1 teaspoon baking soda
2 teaspoons cinnamon
2 teaspoons allspice
2 teaspoons cloves
4 cups all-purpose flour
1 cup buttermilk
2 teaspoons vanilla extract
2 cups raisins
2 cups preserves (peach or pear)
2 cups jam (blackberry)
2 cups nuts

Preheat oven to 300°. Cream together shortening and sugar. Add eggs, one at a time, beating well after each addition. Sift dry ingredients together and blend into shortening mixture. Stir in remaining ingredients. Pour into greased and lined pans. Bake for 30 minutes at 300°. Increase heat to 325° for about 1 hour or until tester inserted in center comes out clean. Wonderful plain or with Caramel Frosting (see recipe on page 165).
*Makes 8 to 10 servings.*

## Strawberry Jam Cake

½ cup solid shortening
1 cup sugar
3 eggs
2 cups all-purpose flour
1 teaspoon cinnamon
¼ teaspoon salt
½ teaspoon nutmeg
½ cup buttermilk
1 teaspoon baking soda
1 cup strawberry jam

Preheat oven to 350°. Cream shortening and sugar until creamy. Add eggs and beat well. Mix flour with spices, salt, and soda. Add to creamed mixture alternately with buttermilk. Stir in jam. Pour into 2 greased and floured 9-inch pans. Bake for 40 to 50 minutes or until tester inserted in center comes out clean. Cool. Frost with favorite icing or topping.
*Makes 10 to 12 servings.*

## Banana Split Cake (Sugar-Free)
*Wilma Fisher*

1 stick diet margarine, melted
2 cups plain graham cracker crumbs
1 15-ounce box sugar-free, fat-free instant pudding
1 20-ounce can unsweetened, crushed pineapple
3 to 4 bananas
1 package Estee Sugar-Free Whipped Topping mix

Mix melted margarine and graham cracker crumbs, press in bottom of 9x13-inch pan. Chill. Prepare pudding mix according to directions. Spread on top of graham cracker crust. Drain pineapple and spread on top of pudding. Slice bananas on top of pineapple. Mix topping mixture as directed. Spread on top. May garnish with chopped pecans, if desired. Chill.
*Makes 8 to 10 servings.*

## Peach Cake
*Betty Givens*

2 eggs
2 cups sugar
1 teaspoon soda
1 teaspoon cinnamon
1 20-ounce can peaches, drained and chopped (½ cup syrup reserved)
2 cups self-rising flour
1 stick butter, melted
½ cup peach syrup

Preheat oven to 350°. Beat eggs; add remaining ingredients. Stir until well blended. Pour batter into a 9x13-inch pan, bake for 35 to 40 minutes.

### Icing
¾ cup sugar
1 stick butter
¾ cup evaporated milk
1 teaspoon milk

Combine all ingredients in saucepan. Cook until mixture coats a spoon, about 5 minutes. Pour over cake while still warm.

# Fruit Cocktail Cake
*Peggy Chapman*

1 cup self-rising flour
1 cup sugar
1 egg
1 16-ounce can fruit cocktail, drained
¼ cup firmly packed brown sugar
½ cup chopped nuts

Preheat oven to 350°. Combine flour, sugar, egg, and fruit cocktail. Pour into greased and floured 9-inch square pan. Sprinkle with brown sugar and nuts. Bake for 1 hour.

# Apricot Nectar Cake
*Elizabeth Wilburn*

1 18½-ounce box lemon cake mix
½ cup sugar
¾ cup vegetable oil
1 cup apricot nectar
4 eggs
1 16-ounce can Betty Crocker creamy deluxe
    butter pecan frosting

Preheat oven to 350°. Lightly grease inside of bundt pan with shortening. Flour lightly. Blend lemon cake mix, sugar, oil, apricot nectar, and eggs, one at a time on low speed for 1 minute, then on medium speed for 2 minutes. Pour batter into bundt pan and bake immediately for 45 to 50 minutes. Do not overbake. Cake is done when tester inserted in center comes out clean. Cool cake about 10 minutes before removing from pan.

Heat frosting in small saucepan over medium heat, stirring constantly, until thin, or microwave opened tub for 20 to 30 seconds or until of spreading consistency. Drizzle over cake while it is still warm.
*Makes 10 to 12 servings.*

# No Bake Fruitcake
*Una Lee James*

¾ cup milk
1 pound marshmallows
1 pound graham crackers
1 pound seedless raisins
1 pint mixed candied fruit
4 cups chopped walnut or pecan meats

Scald milk over low heat; add marshmallows. Stir constantly and cook until smooth. Remove from heat. Crush graham crackers. In large bowl, combine crumbs, raisins, mixed fruits, and nuts. Add marshmallow mixture; blend well (hands are best). Line a 2-quart casserole or mold with wax paper. Add cake mixture; press down firmly so it takes shape of container. Decorate top with candied pineapple, cherries, and almonds. Let cake age at least a month. Saturate a piece of cheesecloth with grape juice and place on top of cake. Wrap in wax paper. Keep refrigerated.
*Makes 10 to 12 servings.*

# White Fruitcake

2 cups sifted all-purpose flour, divided
1 teaspoon baking powder
¼ teaspoon salt
2 sticks butter or margarine, softened
1 cup sugar
5 medium eggs
½ cup dry sherry or orange juice
1 tablespoon lemon juice
1 teaspoon vanilla extract
1½ cups halved candied cherries
1 cup blanched slivered almonds
1 cup light seedless raisins
1 cup candied citron
½ cup diced candied orange peel
1½ teaspoons grated lemon rind
Dry sherry or fruit juice
½ cup apricot preserves, melted
Natural almonds

Generously grease a 10-inch bundt pan. Sift together flour, baking powder, and salt onto a piece of wax paper.

In large bowl with an electric mixer at medium speed, cream together butter and sugar; then beat in eggs until light and fluffy, about 4 minutes. At low speed, alternately blend in 1½ cups flour mixture and sherry, lemon juice, and vanilla.

In another bowl, combine remaining ingredients. Toss fruits and nuts with remaining ½ cup flour mixture, coating evenly. Turn into batter with rubber spatula. Mix until fruits and nuts are evenly distributed.

Preheat oven to 300°. Pour mixture into pan. Bake until tester inserted in center comes out clean, 1 hour and 45 minutes to 2 hours. Cool cake 5 minutes in pan on wire rack. Remove from pan and cool completely. Wrap in sherry or fruit juice-soaked cheesecloth and then in plastic wrap. Store in refrigerator 2 to 3 weeks before serving.
*Makes 10 to 12 servings.*

# Turtle Cake
*Wilma Fisher*

1 18½-ounce box German chocolate cake mix
20 caramels
1 5⅓-ounce can evaporated milk
1 cup chocolate chips
1 cup chopped pecans

Preheat oven to 350°. Mix cake according to directions. Pour 2 cups of cake mix into a greased 9x13-inch pan. Bake for 15 minutes. Remove the pan from the oven. Melt the caramels in milk and pour over baked cake. Sprinkle with chocolate chips. Pour remaining cake batter over top. Sprinkle with pecans. Return to oven and bake for 30 minutes. Remove from oven, cool before cutting.
*Makes 10 to 12 servings.*

# Quick Peach Dessert Cake

4½ cups sliced fresh peaches
½ cup sugar
½ cup butter or margarine, softened
½ cup sugar
1 cup self-rising flour
1 egg
1 teaspoon vanilla extract

Preheat oven to 350°. Place peaches in a lightly greased 8-inch square baking dish. Sprinkle with ½ cup sugar.

Cream butter and ½ cup sugar, beating well. Add flour and egg; mix well. Stir in vanilla extract. Spoon mixture over sugared peaches. Bake for 30 to 35 minutes or until golden brown. *Note:* You can use any kind of fruit desired.
*Makes 6 servings.*

# Chocolate Frosting

4 ounces unsweetened chocolate
1 stick butter
1 pound sifted confectioner's sugar
Dash of salt
1 teaspoon vanilla extract
½ to ⅔ cup evaporated milk

Melt chocolate and butter in double boiler over hot water. Sift sugar and salt together and add the vanilla and chocolate mixture. Add enough milk to make spreading consistency (make sure not to add too much milk). Increase ingredients by ½ to frost a 3 layer cake.
*Makes about 2 cups.*

# Buttercream Frosting

1½ sticks butter or margarine, or ½ of each, softened
6 tablespoons milk
¼ teaspoon salt
2 tablespoons vanilla extract or lemon juice
6¾ cups sifted confectioner's sugar

Place butter, milk, salt, and vanilla in mixing bowl. Add half the sugar, mixing slowly. Gradually add the rest of the sugar. Continue beating until the mixture is light and fluffy. Frosting will be off-white.
*Makes about 2½ cups.*

# Caramel Frosting

¼ cup butter
¾ cup firmly packed light brown sugar
¼ cup evaporated milk
2½ to 3 cups sifted confectioner's sugar
1 teaspoon vanilla extract
Dash of salt

Melt butter in saucepan over medium heat and add brown sugar and milk. Heat until sugar dissolves. Cool slightly, then beat in confectioner's sugar, vanilla, and salt. Double the recipe to frost a 3-layer cake.
*Makes about 1½ cups.*

# Erma's Fudge Icing
*Erma D. Watts*

1 stick margarine
2 cups sugar
½ cup cocoa
½ cup milk
1 teaspoon vanilla extract

Melt margarine in saucepan. Add sugar mixed with cocoa. Pour in milk. Bring to boil. Boil 1 minute. Let cool slightly. Add vanilla. Beat well and pour over cake while it is still warm in the pan.

# $\mathcal{P}$HOTOGRAPHY $\mathcal{C}$REDITS

Berkey, Chris, AP/Wide World Photos, page 3

Graham, Vicki, Fort Worth, TX, pages 9, 13, 26, 44, 46, 52 top, 65, 90, 111

Humphrey, Mark, AP/Wide World Photos, pages 53, 60

Markham, Bill, Carthage, TN, page 73 bottom

Smith County Chamber of Commerce, pages 6, 29, 47 top, 67, 68, 105, 132, 147, 149, 155

Stewart, Doreen, Carthage, TN, pages 78, 98, 154.

*The Tennessean*, Nashville, TN, pages 47 bottom, 58, 65, 101, 108, 114, 116, 118, 140

West, Eddie, *The Carthage Courier*, Carthage, TN, pages xi, 8, 11, 15, 20, 25, 26, 31, 36, 40, 41, 50, 52 bottom, 53, 55, 57, 62, 71, 73 top, 75, 79, 81, 82, 85, 87, 95, 103, 107, 124, 127, 130, 134, 135, 137, 142, 143, 160.

# INDEX

D OREEN STEWART and J ENNIE STEWART are a daughter-and-mother team who have authored two previous cookbooks, *A Dash of Hope and Care* and *Y'All Come for Dinner, We're Cookin' Country*. They are frequent guests on Nashville's *Talk of the Town* television show. Doreen has also written for local newspapers and Jennie has operated a catering service and given seminars on household organization. They both live in Carthage, Tennessee.